Reminiscing In Tempo:
Farewells and Recollections of Showbiz, Jazz, and Drums

BY
BRUCE KLAUBER

LAYOUT AND DESIGN BY STEPHANIE TUJETSCH

ISBN 978-1-57424-357-4

P.O. Box 17878
Anaheim Hills, CA 92817 USA
Phone 714-779-9390
email: centerstrm@aol.com
www.centerstream-usa.com

This book is dedicated to all the beautiful cats who have kept me swingin'.

Acknowledgments

The author would like to gratefully acknowledge *ICON* magazine, *Modern Drummer* magazine and *Broad Street Review* for granting permission to republish the following within this work:

ICON magazine (icondv.com) for use of interviews with Tony Bennett and Harry Connick, Jr., *Playing with Charlie Ventura*, and *Norman Mailer and Charles Mingus.*

Modern Drummer magazine (moderndrummer.com) for use of profiles of drummers Nick Fatool and Rufus Jones, and reviews of *A View From the Back of the Band: The Life and Music of Mel Lewis*, and *Rifftide: The Life and Opinions of 'Papa' Jo Jones.*

Broad Street Review (broadstreetreview.com) for use of the tributes to Ted Gerike, Harry Jay Katz, John Zacherle, Julius LaRosa, Phil Woods, Natalie Cole, Buddy DeFranco, Nat Hentoff, B.B. King, Buddy Rich and reviews of the books *Is That All There Is? The Strange Life of Peggy Lee* and *Just Getting Started by Tony Bennett.*

Special thanks to: Rosina DeLuca for enriching my life and the lives of so many, Andy Kahn and Bruce Kaminsky of The All-Star Jazz Trio, Dan Rottenberg of *Broad Street Review*, Tracy Kearns and Adam Budofsky of *Modern Drummer* magazine, Peggy King, Jordi Pujol of Fresh Sound Records, drummers and archivists Charley Braun, Louis Bernstein and Paul Testa; pianist James Dell'Orefice; singer/bandleader Eddie Bruce; Stephen Yau of Square on Square restaurant; Ron Middlebrook of Centerstream Publishing; and Stephanie Tujetsch, whose superb book design made this book come alive.

Contents

Introduction

Show business, jazz, drums and drumming have been the focal points of my professional life for more than five decades. I've had the good fortune–in retrospect, most of it was good–of working on virtually every side of the entertainment business as a jazz drummer, singer, sometimes saxophonist and vibraphonist, columnist, author, video producer, journalist, talent booker, press agent and publicist. These talents, presuming any talent is involved, must have come from my mother's side of the family. My mother sang and danced in amateur shows in her native Philadelphia, and recorded a demo of "Apple Blossom Time" eight years before the Andrews Sisters had the hit on it. Her sister worked for ASCAP for years and it was said that she knew Jolson. Her brothers sang, and my own brother was a singer and became a respected jazz musicologist.

I was taken to see nightclub shows from a young age and saw the great acts, from Frank and Dean to Sammy Davis and The Three Stooges. My brother and I developed an interest in jazz when I was eight years old, by way of a cousin who had a jazz show on Temple University's radio station. In 1960, WRTI-FM radio couldn't have been heard more than three square miles, but my brother and I tuned in, reception issues notwithstanding, and loved what we heard. The first jazz recordings we ever heard were those of the Benny Goodman band at Carnegie Hall, recorded in January of 1938. The drummer was Gene Krupa.

As for the drums, I was mesmerized when I first saw and heard a kit, owned and played at the time by a friend of my brother's who drummed in the YMHA jazz band. Yes, the YMHA once had a jazz band. The wood, the metal, the shimmering sound of the cymbals, the gold sparkle color and all the other accoutrements were super hip, especially to an eight-year old already in love with show biz and jazz.

It seemed to me that drum lessons were in order, and after a bit of begging, formal study began in 1960, when I was eight years old. My first drum teacher believed that I may have an innate talent, which led to the purchase of the first drum set: The same, gold sparkle rig that my brother's friend played on. Whatever early aptitude for percussion I may have demonstrated was put to the real test not that much longer after my first lesson, when I was called upon to deputize for a drummer in a well-known society orchestra led by a friend of our next door neighbor. The band's drummer had become ill, several hours before the orchestra was scheduled to play a Bar Mitzvah at Philadelphia's Ben Franklin Hotel. The exasperated and hard up bandleader telephoned my parents and asked them if they thought I would want to make the job. No questions were asked about whether or not I had the ability to play the job. I was subsequently dressed in a dark suit, played the gig in a satisfactory manner, and was awarded the grand sum of $45 and a chicken dinner for a four-hour job. As I recall, a lot of Latin music, i.e., cha-chas, merengues and such, was played at this date. I had learned all the beats well.

I continue drumming with as much enthusiasm as ever, and over the years have had the privilege of playing with, as they say, a bunch of "heavy cats," including Charlie Ventura, Milt Bucker, Al Grey, Bernard Peiffer, Pepper Adams, Sonny King, Buddy Greco, Joanie Sommers, Peggy King, Jimmy Bruno and The All-Star Jazz Trio, a unit I co-founded with childhood friend Andy Kahn in 1972, and a group that is still swinging and going strong.

Bruce Klauber, 1966

The writing component of my career came about from a strong suggestion from family that I find something "respectable" to, as they said "fall back on," if full-time drumming did not become a reality. What they did not say, nor did they have to, is that jazz musicians back in the day were not particularly highly thought of as respectable citizens by respectable citizens. I could just hear it: "You're son is a jazz drummer, Mrs. Klauber? My, what a shame."

Demonstrating some facility with spelling and the English language, and having been an avid reader of all those who wrote for *Downbeat* and *Metronome* jazz magazines–Leonard Feather, Martin Williams, George T. Simon, Dan Morgenstern and the rest–it occurred to me sometime in high school that perhaps some type of honest vocation in writing, perhaps with a jazz orientation and coupled with my love of show business in general, might be worth seriously considering.

I like to believe that what ultimately set me apart is that I'm a jazz and show business writer who is also a performer. My goal, as one of the few writers who also performs, is to bring some singular insights about music and the business to the journalistic table. To some extent, I believe I've succeeded.

An interview with Moe Howard of The Three Stooges was published in the *Temple University News* sometime in 1973 and it was the first article I ever wrote that was published. For the past four-plus decades, I've contributed to just about every jazz and percussion journal extant, wrote two well-received books on Gene Krupa, wrote and produced the Warner Bros. and Hudson Music videos on Krupa, Buddy Rich, the *Legends of Jazz Drumming and Classic Drum Solos* series, and a bunch of others; and have written voice over narration for industry giants Ed Bradley, Mel Tormé and Steve Allen. One script I wrote, the Rhythm and Blues Pioneer Foundation's video tribute to R & B trail blazer Louis Jordan, was supposed to be narrated by Maya Angelou and was written just for her. When she dropped out, the great Ed Bradley filled in. Heady company, I'd say.

Though I'm still out there and swinging, I thought this an appropriate time to gather several years of published "remembrances"–of colleagues, musical inspirations, and those I've admired and have known in jazz, drumming and show business through the years–in book form. As detailed herein, these reminiscences were published in *Broad Street Review*, *Jazz Times*, *Modern Drummer* magazine, *ICON* magazine and my long-running *Backstage* columns. And if I might borrow a closing wish from Frank Sinatra, a man I miss as much as my own father, "May you all live to be 1,000 years old, and that the last voice you hear be *mine*."

I

Philly Cats

Philadelphia stands as the birthplace of dozens of world class and internationally known entertainers, jazz musicians, entrepreneurs, media personalities, and like any big city, had its share of real "characters." Herewith are remembrances of a few:

DICK CLARK (1929-2012)

Television host, producer and broadcast pioneer Dick Clark has died at the age of 82.

Clark was one of a handful of Philadelphia-born broadcasters and performers who made it to the national stage–-Ed McMahon, of course, was another–and he pretty much stayed there, front and center, until felled by a stroke in 2004.

Those who knew Clark have been unanimous in their praise of him as a human being, almost granting him saintly status. Entertainer Tony Orlando claims that what you saw in Clark's onstage persona was exactly the way Clark was in real life. Interesting observation. Perhaps Orlando tied too many ribbons around too many old oak trees.

Philadelphia radio host Bob Horn was the creator and first host of Dick Clark's later claim to fame, television's *American Bandstand.* Horn, who hosted from 1952 to 1956, was ousted from that coveted television job due to a drunk driving and statutory rape charge. Though acquitted from the latter, Horn's career was over. Clark replaced him as the host of *American Bandstand* in July of 1956. AB spent a year as a local program emanating from Philadelphia until it was picked up for national broadcast by ABC in 1957. The program lasted, probably too long, in various guises until 1989.

Clark was in the right place at the right time. In the 1950s, certain political powers- that-be in this country were concerned about the newfound popularity of rockers like Elvis, Jerry Lee Lewis, Chuck Berry and the like, because, as we all know, they were all no-account hop-heads who inspired juvenile delinquency. The world, claimed the rock naysayers, needed more personalities like Pat Boone, for Elvis to have his balls cut off by being railroaded into the army, and for a fresh-faced "rock television host" who might somehow put a "safe face" on all this lurid music.

Clark was the guy, and no doubt he was sincere in his passions. So honest-looking and fresh-faced was he, that he escaped the entire payola scandal–paying radio guys for airplay–of the late 1950s. Pioneer rock jock Alan Freed had his career ruined by the scandal. Clark simply said he had no knowledge of any artist or record label that he may have had an interest in being involved in such a terrible affair.

Dick Clark's real contribution to television was as a producer. He was there at the beginning with reality shows, beauty pageants, blooper programs, dozens of game shows, and the legendary New Year's Eve broadcast. None of this was art, nor did it pretend to be. Clark's talent was in making money. Lots of it.

Some years back, I had an idea for a reality television show called *The World's Greatest Drummer*. The weekly series would pit drummers of all ages against one another in competition, playing before celeb/drummer judges like Max Weinberg, Charlie Watts, Ringo, etc. Several production companies were interested, but before seriously proceeding, I wanted to take the concept to "the expert."

While hosting *Bandstand*, Clark had a number of dancers who appeared week after week and ended up with their own followings and fan clubs. One of these vastly popular "regulars" was a West Philly guy named Tommy DeNoble, who eventually had a decent singing career and appeared in a couple of films, including *Ship of Fools*.

I drummed for Tom way back when, and thought that one-time association might help me gain entrance into the offices of "the world's oldest teenager." I sent a note to Clark's office about the reality show concept and association with DeNoble, and lo and behold, Dick Clark himself called me on the telephone.

He was more than nice, stressed that he did not use email and responded to letters with a personal telephone call or letter. He inquired about our mutual friend DeNoble, and then addressed the issue of *The World's Greatest Drummer*. Though he liked the idea, he maintained that because the program was limited to just drums, that the entire concept was just too marginalized to ever reach a wide, general audience. "What would you do as a follow-up?" he asked. "The '*World's Greatest Violin Player*'?"

He was right—at the time, anyway– and I knew it, and I'll never forget that he took the time to respond in the manner he did.

Yes, Clark was in the right place at the right time, and that's great for a start. But he had the vision, strength and determination to succeed, and to succeed for decades in a medium that often spits people out after mere moments is certainly saying something.

More importantly, I think Dick Clark really and truly liked television. It showed. – *Backstage, 2012.*

"FATHER" JOHN D'AMICO (1938-2013)

The job of "house pianist" at the long-running 23rd Street Café' Tuesday night jam session in Philadelphia requires equal amounts of the following: Versatility, creativity, generosity, understanding, good humor, patience, even temperament, positive disposition, and overall, the ability to not take things too seriously.

Pianist Father John D'Amico, who held that piano chair for years and passed away at the age of 74, possessed all those qualities. Those who deemed him "a saint" were pretty accurate, as "Father John," among many other things, was a once a Roman Catholic priest, ordained in 1966.

To play the 23rd Street Café' gig, having a connection to "a higher authority" certainly helped. This isn't your standard jam and never was. On any given evening, Father John—along with his longtime bassist Kenny Davis and Café' session coordinator/drummer "Big" Jim Dofton"– had to back up dozens of singers and instrumentalists of all ages, styles and levels of ability. Anyone with ears who visited or sat in at this Philadelphia institution would be happy to tell you that knowing the song and/or the key that it's in was never a requirement. Still, Father John did it all, Tuesday after Tuesday, making a kid country fiddler or 93-year-old trumpet player sound as good as the various visiting pros who sit in year after year.

The music at the café? Father John would have told you that some of it was great, some of it was near-great, and some of it was not-so-great. Then he would laugh heartily, and move on to back up another singer on yet another version of "Summertime" or "My Funny Valentine."

"Father" John D'Amico

He never judged, never criticized, never gave less than his all, and was always upbeat and encouraging to one and all. Lesser talents and artists of lesser temperaments would have jumped ship from this gig after two weeks. There are a bunch who did. Not Father John.

"He was the kind of person you really liked," his wife of 44 years, Kathleen, told John F. Morrison of the *Philadelphia Daily News*. In a difficult business, there was never, ever a negative word said about Father John D'Amico. In fact, in a career as a piano soloist, bandleader, composer and educator that spanned more than 40 years, the most frequently heard words about him were—and are—"beautiful cat."

His "day gig" was as important to him as his playing. He worked for 23 years as a probation officer for Philadelphia's Court of Common Pleas in the area of drug and rehabilitation, and worked on behalf of a number of charitable causes, many involving the Hispanic community.

As a jazz player, Father John was unique. With his long-time trio members, bassist Kenny Davis and drummer Greg McDonald—and as a solo artist—he was one of the most sensitive and astute interpreters of the music of Thelonious Monk and Bud Powell. But he didn't stop there and continued to evolve stylistically and was, when he wanted to be, as contemporary as any pianist on the scene.

Fortunately, he recorded extensively, worked just about everywhere—including a neat job in Cannes, France--with legends like Lionel Hampton and Philly Joe Jones, and was deservedly the recipient of several honors, including the *John Coltrane Award* for "Outstanding Achievement in Jazz."

The region's jazz scene and jazz community will not be the same without Father John D'Amico. Yes. He was one beautiful cat. – *allaboutjazz.com, 2013.*

ALBERT "TED" GERIKE (1933-2016)

Albert "Ted" Gerike, a beloved fixture on the Philadelphia jazz scene for five decades and the last of the true bebop pianists in the region, died just last week at the age of 83.

He was a gentle, unassuming, supportive man who could and would talk for hours about bop songs, bop players, and compositions from the great American songbook. His knowledge of those topics was encyclopedic. Like the man, his piano style was tasteful, understated, swinging, and inventive. But what listeners, jazz lovers and non-jazz lovers alike could hear in his music was his love and respect for the songs he played and the composers who wrote them.

His following in the Philadelphia area and the sheer length of the jobs he had were unprecedented. After returning from the service in the early 1950s, he was a regular on the nightclub scene, including the long-gone Latin Casino, backing up big names as a part of the house band. When that work dried up, he began an incredible, 22-year residency at the old Society Hill Hotel, where he played six nights per week from 6:00 p.m to 2:00 p.m.

Despite the long hours, he loved it, as did all those regulars and newcomers who heard him. Upon the hotel's policy change – they decided to court a younger audience – he moved to the Prime Rib restaurant in the Warwick hotel, where he was a regular part of the nightly jazz piano rotation; Tuesday was his night. He played there from 2002 until 2014 when he retired, something he did not want to do. The truth is, management was courting a younger clientele and thought that a employing a piano player of a certain age would be demographically off-putting. No matter. As was his wont, however, he still hung out and you never knew just where he would pop up.

Ted Gerike

Stylistically, Gerike could bop with the best of them, coming out of the tradition of jazz piano giants like Bud Powell and Al Haig. What made him so special, and this was likely the reason for his astounding fan base, was his love and respect for the purity of standard tunes as written.

You might say Ted Gerike was a jazzed-up Michael Feinstein. He played the songs – and it's said that even though he did not read music, he knew more than 1,000 of them – but he played them his way. As a performer, he instinctively knew when to play something by Thelonious Monk, and when to play something by Cole Porter.

In 2002, after he was dismissed from the Society Hill Hotel, he did an interview with the *Philadelphia Inquirer*. "I always put the music at the edge of the conversation," he said. "I never wanted people to totally listen to me. If they put me on stage at the Academy of Music and everybody was quiet, I'd freak out."

Jazz pianist, educator, Jacobs Music Artist-in-Residence and my long-time colleague, Andy Kahn, was on that rotation with Ted Gerike at the Prime Rib for several years, and got to know the man and his music. He remembered, "His undeniable total recall of who played with whom, and when, along with his encyclopedic knowledge of the composers of jazz classics and American standards, is legendary."

His ever-swinging, yet always-at-ease style, coupled with his experience as a top-notch pianist and an astonishing chronicler of this music was without parallel. Albert "Ted" Gerike was the last of the certifiable Philadelphia jazz piano beboppers. – *Broad Street Review, 2016.*

HARRY JAY KATZ (1940-2016)

Harry Jay Katz, legendary Philadelphia self-promoter and a character described by the local media for many years as a "man about town," has died at the age of 76. Some people are saddened by this news. Others are not.

Katz was the last in a long line of Philadelphia "characters," including long-forgotten names like Stanley Green and Lillian Reis. Like today's Kardashians, he was more famous for being famous than for having done anything of substance. He had plenty of ideas, to be sure – including opening a Playboy Club in Philadelphia, running a Jewish-styled steak house called Hesch's, resurrecting the Erlanger Theater, and promoting the World Football League –

but none of these enterprises lasted. Those who knew him intimately, as I did, knew that everything would become about Harry rather than the enterprise itself, and that eventually, none of these things would last.

None of them did.

I came to Harry Jay in 1978 from the failing and now-fabled folk coffeehouse in suburban Philadelphia, The Main Point. He had recently started a free weekly newspaper, *ElectriCity*, sort of an updated version of the long-defunct alternative weekly, *The Drummer*, a publication he effectively put out of business when the publication lost a libel suit stemming from a fictitious column he wrote about *Philadelphia Inquirer* columnist Elsa Goss. Harry Jay, always a man of concepts, hooked up with the H.A. Winston hamburger outfit–an innovative restaurant chain with more than a dozen locations that stretched down to Virginia– to distribute the free rag. As for me, it seemed like a good idea at the time and I needed a job. It only took a call to Harry Jay, whom I had known peripherally for years, and who knew me as a writer for the *Drummer*, for him to hire me as music editor.

Harry Jay Katz

It was good for a while, at least for as long as he kept his nose out of things. His then-wife, Andrea Diehl, a fine writer/editor, was the editor of *ElectriCity*. And the ever-enterprising Harry, knowing that everyone wanted to be published, managed to get talents like *Evening Bulletin* theater critic Ernie Schier, *Philadelphia Magazine* film critic Richard Fuller, *Philadelphia Inquirer* classical music writer Tom DiNardo, and bunch of others, to contribute pieces to *ElectriCity* for the grand sum of five dollars per.

One issue, if memory serves, had exclusive interviews with the likes of Phoebe Snow, Buddy Rich, Max Roach, and Bo Diddley.

But inevitably, Harry Jay had to make sure it was destroyed, Buddy Rich and Bo Diddley notwithstanding. He started hiring "columnists" like Frank Stallone; Rita Jenrette, Abscam wife turned *Playboy* model; faded model Apollonia; and just about everyone else who had a history of taking their clothes off in public. And, for reasons better off left undetailed, he instituted the infamous porno-oriented personal ads that were long a fixture of the Drummer. So much for journalistic credibility.

Perhaps the most infamous of our "contributors" was Ira Einhorn, hired by Katz as, if you can believe it, *ElectriCity's* poetry editor – after Holly Maddux's death. Einhorn, who hadn't shaved and showered since 1957, visited me at my office one day. He was shaved, showered, wearing a coat and tie, and looking good. "Who do you think you are, Gregory Peck?" I asked him. "And by the way, where do you think you're going?" He wasn't seen again for years, though the FBI kept our offices at 12th and Spruce Street under surveillance. Harry thought the whole sordid business was just great fun.

A number of things did Harry Jay in, including his 24-hour party-boy lifestyle; his notorious habit of never, ever paying for a product or service; and the brouhaha surrounding the drug- and alcohol-induced death of Valerie Sheridan, whose body was found in the hot tub of Harry Jay Katz's East Falls home.

The reality is, what really did Harry Jay Katz in, is that – as happened with Stanley Green, Lillian Reis, and all the others – history simply passed him by. – *Broad Street Review, 2016.*

JOHN ZACHERLE (1918-2016)

John Zacherle, a.k.a. the "Cool Ghoul" and "Roland," one of Philadelphia's most beloved television and radio personalities, died on October 27, 2016 at the age of 98.

John Zacherle, "The Cool Ghoul"

A native of Germantown and a University of Pennsylvania graduate, Zacherle broke through in the Philadelphia market in 1957. After a couple of stints as a radio and television actor on WCAU TV, he was named as the host named "Roland"–accent on the "*land*"– of late night TV's *Shock Theater.*

Unique for its time, the focus of the program was to have Roland interrupt screenings of grade Z horror pictures with various skits, often involving coffins, severed heads, tombstones and hip asides, all punctuated by his trademark maniacal laugh. All of it, by the way, was unscripted. The bottom line was that Zacherle was hip. Jazz musicians loved him and often tuned him in after their gigs.

Though *Shock Theater* only ran in Philadelphia for 92 broadcasts through 1958, the host was so popular that his local personal appearances, often in tandem with *American Bandstand*'s Dick Clark, drew tens of thousands. Yes, his Top-Ten recording of Cameo Parkway's "Dinner with Drac," was said to be bankrolled by Clark and colorful area clothier Ben Krass. A pre- "Monster Mash" hit, the novelty tune had lyrics such as, "A dinner was served for three/At Dracula's house by the sea/The Hors d'Oeuvres were fine, but I choked on my wine/When I learned that the main course was me!"

He was able to parlay this fame and move *Shock Theater* to a bigger market, New York City's WABC, in 1958. His other gigs in New York throughout the years included hosting a children's cartoon show, a teenage dance program, stints as a morning radio host, and, believe it or not, master of ceremonies at Bill Graham's Fillmore East rock emporium. One can hear his voice introducing the Grateful Dead on the album *Dick's Picks, Volume 4.*

He continued making regular radio, television, and B-movie appearances, and was a major attraction at horror movie conventions, until shortly before his death. He was inducted into Philadelphia's Broadcast Pioneers' Hall of Fame in 2010.

As for his influence, Zacherle was the inspiration for other television horror movie hosts like Elvira – who actually copied the mid-1950s television horror movie hostess Vampira – and Philadelphia TV station WPHL's low-rent Dr. Shock, who attempted to copy Zacherle's makeup and schtick, but without his hipness, intelligence, or class.

Zacherle never claimed to be an innovator, but he was among the first television and radio performers to break down the sacred "fourth wall," make fun of whatever medium he worked in, and generally not take television, radio, or himself seriously. Like David Letterman decades later, Zacherle knew he was on television and made sure the viewer knew he knew it as well.

Further, he was one of the first television performers to demonstrate the power of local television. Sure, there were others before him in our region – think "Pete" Boyle, father of actor Peter Boyle and host of *Chuck Wagon Pete* and *Uncle Pete Presents the Little Rascals* – but only Dick Clark's popularity and transition into a national name rivaled Zacherle's. – *Broad Street Review, 2016.*

PETER NERO AND THE PHILLY POPS DEBACLE

In 2013, pianist/conductor/composer Peter Nero, the man who put The Philly Pops orchestra on the map some 37 years ago, was unceremoniously fired. Because the Pops was in the midst of bankruptcy proceedings, the orchestra's then-new CEO, Frank Giordano, wanted Maestro to take a 40 percent pay cut. Maestro properly refused, with his point being that he was likely the main reason anyone came out to hear the Pops for 35 years.

Peter Nero

After dumping Nero, Giordano promptly hired a journeyman conductor from out-of-town, Michael Krajewski, who also conducts less-than major pops orchestras in Atlanta, Houston, and Jacksonville. This is not to denigrate the talents of Krajewski, but he seemed an odd hire in that he has no name value and no ties to Philadelphia.

Deservedly, Nero wasn't happy about being canned. Those who know him well are aware that he sometimes wears his heart on his sleeve. He voiced his real thoughts about the unfortunate situation to yours truly, then writing for the monthly arts magazine, *ICON*. I won't repeat what he said verbatim, but Maestro knew me as a fellow instrumentalist in addition to being a journalist, and knew I wouldn't write anything out of turn or violate what was told to me in confidence. "I know you're one of the cats," he kindly said.

Unfortunately, Maestro evidently did not realize, in the summer of 2014 when he was interviewed by a reporter from the *Allentown Morning Call*, that said scribe was not "one of the cats." The newspaper quoted Peter Nero directly about the brouhaha:

"They said I was asking for too much money. A bunch of crooks dressed in $3,000 suits came in who didn't know a thing about the music business. They were talking to marketing people who would bring in stick-wavers who would get anything from a third to a quarter of what I got. They didn't care if they got a conductor who played an instrument or not. What they didn't realize is that a large part of the Pop's attraction was my piano playing – it's always been a balancing act between playing and conducting."

Frank Giordano, whose background is in trailer leasing rather than entertainment, was not happy with the piece, specifically the suite remark. Even though Giordano was not referred to by name, he promptly sued Nero for slander, to the tune of one million dollars, despite Maestro's profuse public apology not long after the article appeared.

Giordano claims in the suit, still mired in the courts, that Nero was "obviously referring" to him when he used the word "crook." He didn't mention anything about the price of the suit.

As for the state of things today, the Pops has removed every reference to Peter Nero on its web site and in its program book. But the orchestra continues to do well via vigorous promotion of subscriptions, discounts and an enthusiastic PR department. Musically, the enterprise is less than the stellar gem it was under Nero. Generic concert titles such as "The Music of Billy Joel" and "Broadway's Greatest Hits" are underwhelming, and an organization that once booked guest artists like Mel Tormé, Rosemary Clooney and John Pizzarelli is now using talented but second-line Broadway names like Liz Callaway.

Maestro Nero, now in his 80s, he has returned to his jazz roots and is busier than ever, whether guest starring with symphony orchestras or performing tributes to jazz legend Art Tatum in a duo or trio format. "The Philly Pops thing kept me so busy, that I was doing less and less on the circuit," he told me. "But now, it's starting all over. I'm going back to playing the piano again. People have always written to me during my years with the Pops, saying, 'You don't play enough piano.' So that's what I'm doing."

The Pops' loss, which is considerable, is fortunately jazz's gain. – *"Backstage," 2013.*

II
The Singers

THE KING AND I: PEGGY KING

The legendary jazz songstress known as "pretty, perky Peggy King" had a long and impressive career before and after her mid-fifties tenure on George Gobel's television program.

Cutting her teeth and paying dues at the big band era's end with the ensembles of Charlie Spivak and Ralph Flanagan, King learned her lessons well, parlaying her good looks and fine voice–along with a flair for acting–into an impressive show business resume, which included stints as an MGM contract player and television actress, recording artist, and in-demand nightclub performer who figured prominently in the careers, and sometimes personal lives, of Andre Previn, Bobby Hackett, Charlie Barnet, Harry James, Buddy Rich, Mel Tormé, Sammy Davis, Jr., Bob Hope, and Frank Sinatra. She sang at the Oscars and did Carson show and everything else. Her three years as a co-star on the television program of comic George Gobel continue to be fondly-remembered.

Left to right: Bruce Klauber, Peggy King, Buce Kaminsky, Andy Kahn. Photo: Anthony Dean

In the end, it was her voice: Clean, pure, with perfect intonation, with just enough interpretive turn of phrase to make the composer's message ring true. The composers–all of them–loved her. She respected the melody and respected the lyric.

In the late 1950s, she guested on pianist/composer Bobby Troup's *Stars of Jazz* television program for ABC, and introduced her jazz side. It wasn't a complete changeover. It didn't have to be. More to the point, it was an inflection here and there, a subtle rhythmic emphasis on a word or a phrase to get the message across. Her gentle sense of swing had your finger popping when you least expected it. It was the same on ballads. She knew the drama was already in there, and that her job was only to bring it out.

The recordings? There were hundreds of them. All glorious, despite material that was sometimes not up to her standards.

Then there was nothing. Or at least not much. The slowdown, which began in 1961 with her marriage to After Six formal wear founder Sam Rudofker, was gradual. It was time for a family, and while there were still songs and plenty of them, they eventually slowed to a trickle. By the 1980s, there was the odd benefit here and there near her suburban Philadelphia home, but not much. Perhaps she was intuitive enough, circa 1961, to see the handwriting that would end up on the wall as it related to singers of popular songs, however jazzy.

None of this escaped the Philadelphia promo dynamo, Anthony DiFlorio. DiFlorio, known as "Anthony DiFlorio III" by his intimates, learned showbiz at the knee of another area icon, the late Atlantic City broadcaster Sonny Schwartz. In terms of entertainment, DiFlorio learned what worked and what didn't, who was good, who was not and why, the value of pacing, and how to hype the living heck out of everything.

In years since, he has become a respected pop culture historian, and world class publicist of all things pre-Lady Gaga. Don't be fooled. DiFlorio knows plenty.

He loved Peggy King. Always did. When he found out she was still in the Philadelphia area and no longer singing, coupled with the knowledge that reissues of her old product were coming fast and furious in Japan and points overseas, he was determined to get her out there again. He did facilitate appearances here and there where she sang a tune or two, but there was nothing lasting.

Until 2013.

It started innocently and coincidentally. My longtime personal and professional colleague, the pianist/singer/composer/record producer Andy Kahn and I, reunited and put together our once regionally famed trio–The All-Star Jazz Trio–after a 40-year layoff. We were astonished and pleased to find ourselves, older and wiser after working together for more than 50 years, hotter than we've ever been.

With an assist from the regional arts/music/pop culture magazine ICON, as well as WRTI Radio, Jacobs Music and The Chamber Orchestra of Philadelphia, our All-Star Jazz Trio organized a benefit for the non-profit music ed organization, Musicopia. The All-Star's long-time bassist Bruce Kaminsky, a part of Musicopia for more than a decade, helped institute the hook-up.

The event, held early in the summer of 2013, featured the cream of area classical and jazz players, including our trio, and was a sell-out.

It goes without saying that Anthony DiFlorio was on the press list and was invited. He called and asked if he could bring Peggy King as a guest. I had done a benefit with King at Combs College of Music in the mid-1980s, always admired her, and happily told DiFlorio I looked forward to seeing her and hoped she would enjoy the show.

She showed up, very pretty and perky. I introduced her from the stage. The crowd went crazy when they heard her name and she stood up, and after our hour program, autograph seekers and well-wishers surrounded her for a good 45 minutes. Amidst the excitement and glory, she made time to talk to us, and her words made all the work, sweat and effort that went into putting this show on more than worthwhile. More importantly, what she said about us musically made plenty of sense. The words were very kind, but they were very intelligent, and they were words that could have only come from a pro.

We left the gig with hugs and kisses and her promise that "we must do something together." It appears we inspired her. All-Stars pianist Andy Kahn was excited about the prospect of doing "something together." I was also, and evidently, Peggy King was, too. As for Anthony DiFlorio III, he just smiled. He knew this might happen.

Given that Peggy King, like Tony Bennett, are of a certain age, the concern was not whether she wanted to sing but whether she could, having admitted that she hadn't really sung in about a dozen years. After the first of many telephone conversations with her, Kahn—who started in this business as a child actor and can sense such things—said he was certain she could sing.

We had a get together at Kahn's Philadelphia home, and there was Peggy, standing up next to the piano and singing better than anyone one-third her age. The time, intonation, purity, sincerity, interpretive powers, subtle sense of swing, dynamics, and range were all there, and in some ways, better than they were in 1955. On a personal basis, she regaled us with her knowledge of songs and their writers, of the business, and mostly, of the songs. And her lovely words to us only made us play better. She appreciated that we knew what she considers the lost art of "accompanying."

The All-Stars had an upcoming gig at Chris' Jazz Café', one of Philadelphia's only "name" jazz clubs and the second oldest jazz room in the nation. Days before that job, we let it be known to the press and public that the one and only Peggy King was going to "guest star" at Chris' with us. Word travels quickly in Philadelphia. When we arrived at Chris', you would have thought you were at Grauman's Chinese for a movie premier, what with all the autograph seekers, flashes from still cameras and those holding video rigs.

This woman—this exquisite, graceful, professional *artist*—sang so, so beautifully. It wasn't a question of "still having it." "It," that indefinable "it" was always there. It had to be. No, on a professional level, perhaps she didn't need to sing for all those years. But it was clear that her soul needed it. And wanted it.

We didn't want to tax her or take advantage, so we only asked her to join us for several numbers in the second half of our first show. She insisted on staying and participating in our second show, which went rather late into the night. She had more energy than all of us. Combined. Her version of "Little Girl Blue," worked out quickly with Andy Kahn during the break, brought tears to my eyes. And a lot of others. This was Peggy King. Rather, this *is* Peggy King, and it's a beautiful friendship that has now lasted four years.

Andy Kahn, our bassist Bruce Kaminsky and yours truly have been blessed with the honor and privilege of backing some of the certifiable instrumental and vocal jazz stars though the years. There have been hundreds of them. But none of them—none of them—were like Peggy King. - *Notes to the Fresh Sound Records CD "Peggy King and The All-Star Jazz Trio: Songs ala King," 2015.*

Note: In the summer of 2017, Peggy King decided to withdraw from public performing. It is the music business' loss. And ours.

JULIUS LAROSA (1930-2016)

Singer Julius LaRosa, who passed away at the age of 86 and had close ties to Philadelphia via his many appearances with The Philly Pops and in the Atlantic City casinos, will forever be remembered as the guy who, in 1953, was fired by television/radio icon Arthur Godfrey on the air.

That's unfortunate, as LaRosa was not only one of the most literate entertainers in the industry – he would have been a great writer if he hadn't been a singer – but spoke eloquently about the art of singing and how difficult it was to be an Italian/American vocalist and *not* sound like Frank Sinatra.

It was a challenge, but he did it and did it well, and ultimately became an original, jazz-oriented stylist, whose choice of material was singular and eclectic, way before names like Harry Connick Jr., Michael Bublé, and the rest came to the forefront. And though he sang some Sinatra songs, he sounded *nothing* like Mr. Sinatra. Pianist/conductor Peter Nero, the deposed Philly Pops Maestro, loved LaRosa's work and booked him often. One of LaRosa's final Pops appearances also included jazz guitarist/vocalist John Pizzarelli on the bill, and these guys swung their individual and collective cans off.

However, he knew that whatever or wherever the gig was, interviewers were going to ask him about the Godfrey brouhaha from decades ago.

It is important to remember that in the early 1950s, Arthur Godfrey was the biggest entertainer in the country, with several top-rated television and radio shows, and an estimated 12 percent of the CBS network's advertising revenue. "The old redhead," as he was called, was noted for his folksy, natural and supposedly honest approach to broadcasting – if he didn't like a sponsor's product, he said so – and was fond of saying that the many singers and entertainers in his television cast were "family." The truth was that Godfrey was a jealous, arrogant, petty, and vindictive boss, and an alleged anti-Semite to boot, who would not tolerate any member of his beloved "family" who got more attention than he did.

Julius LaRosa, 1953

Godfrey first heard LaRosa when LaRosa was in the Navy. Impressed, he hired him for both his television and radio program upon his discharge, and ultimately, the singer became the star of Godfrey's programs from 1951 to 1953. After a hit record or two, LaRosa's popularity grew, and the singer did the unthinkable. He hired his own agent.

This didn't sit well with Godfrey. On October 19, 1953, La Rosa was due to begin the TV portion of Godfrey's show but was kept waiting backstage until the final minutes of the radio-only part of the program. As he finished singing "Manhattan," La Rosa and the audience heard Godfrey precede his sign-off by saying, "That was Julie's swan song with us." A few days later, Godfrey said he fired his vocalist because he lacked "humility" and because he had hired an agent.

In the aftermath, LaRosa's celebrity grew, while Arthur Godfrey's career was never the same.

The singer continued appearing on television and in live stage shows, but things eventually died down. He became a successful disc jockey on a major New York radio station, and performed live in New York City, Las Vegas, and other cities.

When I had the good fortune of getting to know him, he had made peace with the Godfrey nonsense. "Of course that's what interviewers are going to ask me," he said, and he knew exactly where he stood within the music business. In our final conversation, we discussed the business climate for artists like him, Vic Damone, Jack Jones, Frank Sinatra Jr., Steve Lawrence, and other superior Great American Songbook interpreters. "It used to be that all of us were thrilled if we filled a 450-seat house," he said. "Today, if you can't fill a 20,000-seat stadium, you won't even be considered."

Julius LaRosa should be considered. He was one of those very, very few in the industry about whom you never heard a bad word. He was a fine singer and a fine man. – Broad Street Review, 2016

Peter Nero Remembers Julius LaRosa

Singer Julius LaRosa was a frequent guest of The Philly Pops during Peter Nero's long tenure there. Maestro Nero, who by all rights should still be conducting the Pops, was kind enough to share his personal remembrances of Julie for "Backstage."

I had won the Godfrey Show (Arthur Godfrey's Talent Scouts on a CBS-TV and radio network simulcast) in June of 1954. One of the prizes offered was a week on his network radio show. The McGuire Sisters were regulars. We were all in the Green Room which was about 100 feet from the studio where Godfrey held court and the audience paid homage. We all sat apprehensively, waiting to be called to do our turn. Once called, we rocketed down the hallway and arrived at breathlessly at the studio as the band played our intro and we stumbled into our places. I was told that's the way the way Godfrey wanted it: "made it exciting". Our performances weren't enough, I guess, to engender "excitement."

Godfrey was nice to me, so at that time I had no idea what he had done to Julie. Firing him on the air was bad enough but the real reason was worse: he didn't want Julie to succeed unless it was on his show and while Julie was on his way to further stardom (he had signed with an artist manager and Godfrey was furious. I know this because Julie told me so.), and Arthur had lost control.

The Philly Pops was born in 1979 and I was the Founding Music Director and Conductor. Julie was a guest artist with us in the mid 1980s and he was sensational! An obvious Sinatra devotee he nevertheless had enough of his own style honoring the tradition of the quintessential big band vocalist.

Backstage we had a chance to chat and he gave me a detailed firsthand account of that which led to his demise. I thought that the event that triggered his on-the-air firing was bad but didn't realize how bad it really was. When I announced his name at the top of the concert I expected the usual rousing reception our audiences gave to our guest artists. To my surprise I was flabbergasted at the (at best) lukewarm reception and was afraid of where it would from there. I'm happy to state that it was all roses after that and Julie wowed them. Finally.

He had warned me of the effect that fateful pronouncement had on his life and career but I didn't believe it until I had experienced it. Four great concerts, all following the same scenario. He won the battle but had to work hard to overcome the stigma cast upon his career.

Several years later singer Margaret Whiting was a scheduled guest. The night before the rehearsal we got a call that she had busted her ankle crossing Fifth Avenue that day. Countless phone calls with no results for a last minute substitute and suddenly someone suggested Julie. He accepted and it was now on to the next chapter.

Julie had a hearing problem which affected many singers as well other musicians. The culprit being the bands that would play loud enough to crack the plaster on the walls in the concert hall. I was only hoping that it hadn't gotten worse over the few years that had passed since we had worked with him. However, with the Philly Pops they knew enough to modulate the volume so that there would be no casualties. Add that factor together with the fact that Julie was wearing not one but two hearing aids. Happy to state that all went better than ever.

One note of levity: singers are notorious for forgetting lyrics and yet the audience never notices. I empathize with them since being an instrumentalist I'm not really listening to the words; just the music. Julie pulled off what I consider the best recovery from a potential show-stopping disaster. He was barely into the Gershwin song "Summertime" and was singing "Summertime, and the livin' is easy......... Fish are jumpin (should now be "and the cotton is high") and he went blank. I mentally gasped as he made an ever-so slight pause and then came up with "as they look to the sky..."

It's difficult to get weak in the knees when you're sitting at a piano but it happened. I had difficulty controlling myself and thought I would have to leave the stage but the moment (which seemed like a lifetime) passed and all returned to normal.

We'll miss you, Julie. You won the battle and went on to share your talents with an adoring public and were always the gentleman.

R.I.P., Julius LaRosa. – *Broad Street Review, 2016.*

PETER NERO REMEMBERS JULIUS LAROSA

Singer Julius LaRosa was a frequent guest of The Philly Pops during Peter Nero's long tenure there. Maestro Nero, who by all rights should still be conducting the Pops, was kind enough to share his personal remembrances of Julie for "Backstage."

I had won the Godfrey Show (*Arthur Godfrey's Talent Scouts* on a CBS-TV and radio network simulcast) in June of 1954. One of the prizes offered was a week on his network radio show. The McGuire Sisters were regulars. We were all in the Green Room which was about 100 feet from the studio where Godfrey held court and the audience paid homage. We all sat apprehensively, waiting to be called to do our turn. Once called, we rocketed down the hallway and arrived at breathlessly at the studio as the band played our intro and we stumbled into our places. I was told that's the way the way Godfrey wanted it: "made it exciting". Our performances weren't enough, I guess, to engender "excitement."

Godfrey was nice to me, so at that time I had no idea what he had done to Julie. Firing him on the air was bad enough but the real reason was worse: he didn't want Julie to succeed unless it was on his show and while Julie was on his way to further stardom (he had signed with an artist manager and Godfrey was furious. I know this because Julie told me so.), and Arthur had lost control.

The Philly Pops was born in 1979 and I was the Founding Music Director and Conductor. Julie was a guest artist with us in the mid 1980s and he was sensational! An obvious Sinatra devotee he nevertheless had enough of his own style honoring the tradition of the quintessential big band vocalist.

Backstage we had a chance to chat and he gave me a detailed firsthand account of that which led to his demise. I thought that the event that triggered his on-the-air firing was bad but didn't realize how bad it really was. When I announced his name at the top of the concert I expected the usual rousing reception our audiences gave to our guest artists. To my surprise I was flabbergasted at the (at best) lukewarm reception and was afraid of where it would from there. I'm happy to state that it was all roses after that and Julie wowed them. Finally.

He had warned me of the effect that fateful pronouncement had on his life and career but I didn't believe it until I had experienced it. Four great concerts, all following the same scenario. He won the battle but had to work hard to overcome the stigma cast upon his career.

Several years later singer Margaret Whiting was a scheduled guest. The night before the rehearsal we got a call that she had busted her ankle crossing Fifth Avenue that day. Countless phone calls with no results for a last minute substitute and suddenly someone suggested Julie. He accepted and it was now on to the next chapter.

Julie had a hearing problem which affected many singers as well other musicians. The culprit being the bands that would play loud enough to crack the plaster on the walls in the concert hall. I was only hoping that it hadn't gotten worse over the few years that had passed since we had worked with him. However, with the Philly Pops they knew enough to modulate the volume so that there would be no casualties. Add that factor together with the fact that Julie was wearing not one but two hearing aids. Happy to state that all went better than ever.

One note of levity: singers are notorious for forgetting lyrics and yet the audience never notices. I empathize with them since being an instrumentalist I'm not really listening to the words; just the music. Julie pulled off what I consider the best recovery from a potential show-stopping disaster. He was barely into the Gershwin song "Summertime" and was singing "Summertime, and the livin' is easy......... Fish are jumpin (should now be "and the cotton is high") and he went blank. I mentally gasped as he made an ever-so slight pause and then came up with "as they look to the sky..."

It's difficult to get weak in the knees when you're sitting at a piano but it happened. I had difficulty controlling myself and thought I would have to leave the stage but the moment (which seemed like a lifetime) passed and all returned to normal.

We'll miss you, Julie. You won the battle and went on to share your talents with an adoring public and were always **the gentleman.**

R.I.P., Julius LaRosa. – *Broad Street Review, 2016.*

NATALIE COLE (1950-2015)

Any number of rockers, folkies, and posters have made attempts, however sincere, to sing songs from the Great American Songbook.

Linda Ronstadt, who made three albums of standards with arranger Nelson Riddle (*What's New* in 1983, *Lush Life* from 1984, and *For Sentimental Reasons* from 1986), probably sold the most recordings, though the trend actually started in 1981, with folky Carly Simon's unfortunate Torch. These days, the unlikeliest of artists are singing the songs of Cole Porter, among others, including Rod Stewart, Barry Manilow, and, of all people, Paul McCartney. The results, we shall say, have been mixed.

Natalie Cole, however, was, the real thing. It helped, perhaps, that she grew up in a household filled with some of the finest music imaginable – that of her father, the beloved singer/pianist Nat "King" Cole.

Whatever she heard or whatever her influences were, Natalie – like many musicians who came of age in the 1960s – fell under the spell of Aretha Franklin and other R&B artists. After she graduated from the University of Massachusetts, she recorded a few R&B demos but literally couldn't give them away until they came to the attention of her dad's old record label, Capitol. Released in 1975, Natalie Cole's first album, *Inseparable*, won a Grammy for Best Female R&B Vocal Performance.

Natalie Cole

Other chart-topping hits followed, and some began calling her "the new Aretha," much to the displeasure of Ms. Franklin. Personal and professional ups (including a hit version of Bruce Springsteen's "Pink Cadillac") and downs (struggles with substance abuse and a six-month stint in rehab) ensued. In 1991, however, Natalie not only resurrected her career but also totally switched musical gears by turning to her father's songbook.

Previously, Natalie Cole had refused to sing any of her father's songs in concert or on record. Whether it was a marketing ploy, a heartfelt choice, or a combination of both, *Unforgettable: With Love* sold more than seven million copies and was Grammy's Album of the Year. (Her posthumous duet with her dad on the title song was Grammy's Song of the Year.) She went on to make several more albums of standards and covers, plus numerous Christmas albums, sometimes with her uncle, singer Freddy Cole, on piano.

What set Natalie Cole apart from the other popsters trying to make like Frank Sinatra or Tony Bennett was her depth, her sincerity, and her understanding of the lyric and where it came from –which came, in part, so it seems, from her father's example. She not only touched audiences familiar with the Songbook classics, but helped younger audiences appreciate this music as well. She also opened the door to the various rock stars and their albums of standards, as well as Lady Gaga's duets with Tony Bennett.

The difference is that listeners knew Natalie Cole was expressing genuine emotion and that the magic, which is what it was, was coming from a credible place. Whatever one's feelings are about Frank Sinatra Jr., audiences instinctively know that they are hearing something as close to the real thing as there is. He is, after all, Frank Sinatra's son. And Natalie Cole? She was, after all, Nat "King" Cole's daughter. – *Broad Street Review, 2015.*

"IS THAT ALL THERE IS? THE STRANGE LIFE OF PEGGY LEE"

The late songstress Peggy Lee was, by all accounts, a certifiable piece of work. However difficult, cruel, temperamental, and downright wifty she might have been, the "queen of the supper clubs" nevertheless was a supremely talented singer and lyricist, and her body of work, created over five decades, certainly qualifies her as a show business legend.

There have been a few books written about Peggy Lee – Miss Peggy Lee, as she insisted upon being called – including her own glossy and inaccurate autobiography, first published in 1989 and republished in 2002. But James Gavin's new book, *Is That All There Is? The Strange Life of Peggy Lee* (Simon and Schuster) is, without a doubt, definitive.

Gavin, who also wrote superb bios of Lena Horne and Chet Baker, is meticulous in his detail and in his research, and he apparently spoke to just about every musician, friend, colleague, and family member still living. What emerges here is a portrait of a very talented and unique innovator who was also very, very disturbed.

Born Norma Deloris Egstrom in Jamestown, North Dakota, she had a childhood that, by all accounts, wasn't easy, but, Gavin says, was nowhere near the terribly abusive one she claimed to have had at the hands of her stepmother. Lee created a lot of myths over the years; this was the biggest.

Whatever hurt was deeply buried within her, and whatever the cause, it affected her personal and professional life, to say nothing of her always fragile health, for years. Among other things, she was married and divorced four times, was an alcoholic and abuser of prescription drugs, a hypochondriac, an inveterate litigator, a control freak with little regard or loyalty to the people who worked for her for years, and a true eccentric who often appeared to be, quite simply, in a fog. You've got to figure something is amiss with someone who stays in bed for years at a time.

Despite all of that, there were the songs she sang and the lyrics she wrote, and that is what she'll be remembered for. And that is as it should be. Her professional breakthrough came with Benny Goodman's band in 1941; she had her first hit record the following year and had a megahit in the form of "Why Don't You Do Right?" a year later. And the hits kept coming, songs like "Mañana," "Lover," "Fever," and 1968's "Is That All There Is?" Though her voice got smaller through the years – and it never was a big instrument to begin with – she always showed the direct influence of Billie Holiday, albeit a stripped down and more erotic-sounding Lady Day.

As a lyricist, Lee will likely be best remembered for her contributions to Disney's Lady and the Tramp and songs like "It's a Good Day," "I Love Being Here with You," and "I'm Gonna Go Fishin'," the latter composed with Duke Ellington.

She was also quite the industry pioneer. Lee was among the first woman to write for films, helped create the "concept album," and, in her lawsuit filed against Disney (Disney was not paying any additional royalties to Lee when *Lady and the Tramp* was released on home video), forever changed the way that musical artists were compensated for their work.

Though not a musician, the author deserves credit for his observations about Lee's musicality as well as the singular contributions of her accompanists – who were some of the greatest jazz musicians who ever lived. Painstakingly researched and beautifully written, *Is That All There Is?* is at times touching, sad, disturbing, and hilarious. Just like Peggy Lee.

The one minor error I could find actually has to do with Philadelphia. Peggy Lee was a regular at our very own Latin Casino, but the author places Lee's 1958 Latin Casino appearance in Cherry Hill when it was still at 13th and Walnut Street. These things happen. – *Broad Street Review, 2014.*

INTO THE FOG WITH MEL TORMÉ (1925-1999)

Left to right: Mel Tormé, Peggy Lee, Buddy Rich, circa late 1960s.

Mel Tormé, is rarely spoken of these days. And that's a crime as, possibly along with Sammy Davis, Jr., Mel Tormé was the most talented individual in the history of show business. He brought an artistic intellect and sensibility to everything he did, which is something I don't believe others did. On a personal basis, he gave me credibility via his contributions to my books and videos through the years, and that's something you don't forget. Was he a genius? Absolutely. Was he eccentric? Certainly. Geniuses are entitled to be eccentric.

After my first video on Gene Krupa came out courtesy of DCI Music Video/Warner Bros. Publications, and did, so they told me, very well, the next logical choice for the subject of a video was Buddy Rich. Choosing a narrator for this project was obvious. Mel Tormé had been one of Buddy Rich's closest friends for almost 40 years. Additionally, Tormé had written the introduction to my first book on Gene Krupa, and was very complimentary about the newspaper and magazine stories I wrote about him through the years.

The problem was that Tormé, at the time, was not getting along with one of the principals involved in our prospective production. I took my issue to him personally, during one of his then-annual appearances at Michael's Pub in New York City. After his show, while he was quickly going through a box of jelly doughnuts, I asked him what I should do.

"You're the only guy for this, Mel, but you don't get along with one of our people, so what do I do?"

"Kid, this has to be done, and you're the one to do it. I'll do it." And like Steve Allen, he did it for a $500 "honorarium."

I started writing the script for what would turn out to be a two-volume set on Buddy Rich, with participation of the Rich family and some of the legendary drummers–old and young–in the business. I called Mel Tormé when the script was ready, and came up with an idea for a cost-cutting measure. Trying to avoid the costs of traveling to Beverly Hills, I figured that a guy of Tormé's stature and artistry would surely have some kind of pro recording set-up in his home. And remember, this was only a voice recording, so it was no big deal. Or so I thought.

I was correct, according to Mel, who proudly detailed all the high-end recording equipment he had in his home. I called him when I believed he had received the script and asked him when he could start. Though he said he loved my script--I've always tried to write in the "voice" and the attitude of the narrator--he voiced concern about the whereabouts of his 500 bucks.

"We sent it out two weeks ago," I told Tormé.

"Wait, kid," he said. "Hold on."

I waited a good six minutes holding the phone while Mel Tormé rooted around his Beverly Hills mansion for a $500 check. He finally found it and let me know he intended to start recording his narrative right away.

Ten or so days later, all of us—DCI Music Video's' Rob Wallis, Paul Siegel and an editing genius and Oscar nominee Phil Fallo—were at the NVI production studios in New York, and we were eagerly anticipating delivery of Mel Tormé's narration, recorded at his state-of-the-art home studio.

The envelope, with several other names and addresses crossed out on it—including that of Jimmy Stewart—finally arrived. Within was one of those made-in-Mexico, nickel tape cassettes that used to be sold at ten for a dollar at Woolworth's. My heart was sinking. Rob, Paul and Phil were giggling. Phil took the tape and inserted it into one of NVI's truly state-of-the-art tape machines.

My suspicions were confirmed. Tormé's narration sounded as if it was recorded in a "make your own record" booth at a carnival. It was not usable, and my colleagues were now in gales of laughter. I had to come up with a plan. How do you tell a big time celebrity that his work, for which he was paid a tiny amount, is no good? The answer was to play on the ego of Mel Tormé, which was enormous.

I called Tormé in Beverly Hills and told him we received the tape. "Mel, I said, "Your narration is so emotional and so heartfelt that you had all of us in tears up here. It's a remarkable performance that cries out to be recorded on an MGM sound stage."

"You're right, kid," he said.

I was off the hook and in a few days, found a good recording studio near Tormé's home. The time was booked and was seemingly okay with Mel. Strangely, he asked me to call him at home and wake him up an hour before the studio was booked. He cancelled three times, but finally got a superb Mel Tormé performance on tape.

Several months later, the two volume video set, *Buddy Rich: Jazz Legend*, was released. I consider it my finest work thus far. Buddy was the idol of everyone who ever played, or wanted to play the drums. Technically, what he could do on a drum set was simply inhuman. I loved the man, and to have the opportunity to work with his family, friends and colleagues was, to me, a dream. I only wish Bud could have lived to see it.

I once asked Buddy's daughter, Cathy, an integral part of this whole project, what her father would have thought of it. "He would have loved it," she said.

Shortly after the videos were released, my friend Louis Bernstein called me at home. Louis and I have been friends since we were kids. Not only is he a great drummer, but at the time, knew more about Buddy Rich than almost anyone. He was also acquainted with Mel Tormé, as Louis often provided Mel's drummer, Donny Osborne, with his own, Buddy Rich-type set of Rogers drums. On the phone, Louis told me that Mel Tormé had called him, asking him to tell me to call him. Got that?

"Why is he calling you to call me to tell me to call him?" I asked.

"Figure it out, Bruce," Louis said. "He called me at work because we have a toll-free, 800 number."

Oh.

I got Mel on the phone. He said he was out on the road and wanted ten copies of each volume of *Buddy Rich: Jazz Legend* and he wanted them delivered the next day.

I told him I'd take care of it, although I wasn't sure how. I reached the offices of our distributor, Warner Bros. Publications, in Miami, and let them know this absolutely had to be done. They balked a bit because of cost—each video sold for $39.95 back then—but when I stressed the importance of this favor, they went for it.

Two days later, Louis Bernstein called me again, and told me in no uncertain terms that I had to call Mel Tormé immediately, and that Mel "was not happy." This was not good.

I called Mel and he was ballistic. "I got this box up here from Miami and I counted only nine copies of one of the video volumes. I specifically asked for ten of each. I am not happy. I am not happy. I am not happy."

He wasn't. I carefully explained how difficult this was to put together for him on such short notice, that Warner Bros., not me, was responsible for the error, and told him how much his friendship and support meant to me personally and professionally over the years. I told him he was responsible for my career. I told him he was a genius. He finally calmed down. And yes, we did overnight him the "missing" volume. Incidentally, let the record show that what I told him about his friendship, support and what he did on my behalf were words that came from the heart.

Though he did not drink or smoke, Mel Tormé had a debilitating stroke in 1996 which ended his performing career. He died in 1999. It's a shame he passed when he did. He was singing better than he ever, and by way of his appearances on the popular television show, *Night Court*, and the commercials he did for Mountain Dew, he was finally beginning to get the national attention and recognition that he craved, without ever compromising his high musical standards. Was he eccentric? Certainly. But I think a man of his talents was entitled to be.

Note: These days, there are a lot of quasi-tribute shows out there, featuring cut-rate performers impersonating Sinatra and various other famed singers. Given his singular talents, Mel Tormé is not an artist easily impersonated or even channeled. But some years after Mel's death, I met up with his son, Steve March Tormé, who was on tour, performing a singing tribute to his father. His interpretations of his father's legendary work with The Marty Paich Dek tette and other arrangers were absolutely flawless. If Steve is singing in your neck of the woods, make it a point to hear him. – *Not So Modern Drummer magazine, 2000*

"JUST GETTING STARTED," BY TONY BENNETT

Though his vocal ability has fallen off slightly over the past few years, 90-year old Tony Bennett is singing remarkably well and continues with a punishing schedule of concert appearances and recordings. Needless to say, in his six-plus decades as an entertainer, he's met entertainment royalty and has been fortunate enough to call a number of those legends–from Sinatra and Nat Cole to Ellington and Basie–his personal friends.

Bennett has written several books over the years, including a somewhat candid autobio called *The Good Life*. His latest, *Just Getting Started* (HarperCollins) pays tribute to many of those who inspired him, including, surprisingly, names like Dr. Martin Luther King, Jr., Amy Winehouse, Jackie Kennedy and Charlie Chaplin. Generally, while certainly a charming read, Tony Bennett shouldn't think seriously about abandoning the singing gig.

Being a tremendous talent, in this case as a musical artist and a painter, does not guarantee that said artist has a tremendous amount of insight. Those who have interviewed Bennett and/or have spent time with him through the years, including yours truly, are well aware that publicly, he does not have a critical word about anyone. While that's all well and good, it does not make for compelling reading or a compelling interview and it's pretty clear that he's said most of these things before.

As an example, Tony Bennett was one of the few who really knew the virtually unknowable Duke Ellington. Not long ago, I tried getting Bennett to open up about the "real" Duke, but he ended up repeating most of the party lines that have been said for years about Duke's writing for specific members of his orchestra, etc. No, there's little doubt that this man knows his jazz–he recorded two, duo albums with legendary pianist Bill Evans as an example–but he offers few new insights about his friends and mentors in *Just Getting Started*.

By and large, Bennett offers expanded bios of his heroes, which could have been cribbed from Wikipedia, as well as an anecdote or two about those he's met personally. However, to give credit where credit is due, there are several touching and heartfelt tributes within, notably to pianist Bill Evans, his tragic recording partner Amy Winehouse, his own mother and father, and a long overdue tribute to his longtime accompanist/ musical director, the late Ralph Sharon. And truth be told, Bennett made musical life difficult more than once for the gentle Sharon over the years. The book is also nicely illustrated with reproductions of Tony Bennett paintings. Yes, he's good.

Tony Bennett

If one is interested in the "real" Bennett, beyond the sweetness and light, it's best to check out the bio, *All The Things You Are: The Life of Tony Bennett*, written by one-time *Paris Review* senior editor David Evanier. Among other things, Evanier tells of Bennett's ban on Ralph Sharon's use of minor chords and his edict to drummer Louie Bellson that he cease playing the hi-hat cymbal on beats "two" and "four"–making it virtually impossible to play– and paranoia about, yes, his nose.

Bottom line for Bennett fans who are considering reading this book is that it's about the music, not whether or not Jimmy Durante once patted him on the head in 1957.– *Broad Street Review, 2016.*

AN INTERVIEW WITH TONY BENNETT

Tony Bennett, 87 years of age when this interview was conducted, is still as enthusiastic–or maybe even more enthusiastic–about jazz, jazz musicians and singing than when I first met him in 1970. I was but a wee lad back then, playing drums in Philadelphia with sax great Charlie Ventura. One evening, the wonderful jazz pianist–John Bunch–newly-appointed Musical Director for Tony Bennett and former Ventura cohort in the Gene Krupa Jazz Quartet, walked in after his Bennett gig and wanted to sit in. I'll never forget it.

All Bunch wanted to talk about was how much he loved and respected his new boss, and how much patience and trust Bennett had with him, given that John Bunch never, to use his words, "musically directed for anyone." Bunch got Ventura and me in to see Bennett later that week, and I met him after the show at the late and lamented Latin Casino in Cherry Hill, New Jersey.

The second time I got to "hang with the master," as it were, was during a Tony Bennett appearance in southwest Florida. After his marvelous, sold-out show, we caught up on matters about his current rhythm section, how much he missed John Bunch, who had recently passed away, and just how important drummers were to his music and his own personal heartbeat. He could not say enough about Harold Jones, his drummer then and now. "You know," he said, "I'll never forget what my good friend Count Basie said to me years ago. Count said that no matter how many cats may be in the band, it's the drummer that's the leader, and I've had the luck to work with the best of them, just like my man, Harold Jones."

With the advent of The Beatles, the music business changed. Bennett, along with other quality singers, was asked by his record company to do covers of juvenile pap. Though he tried valiantly, Bennett just could not and would not sell out, and he departed Columbia Records in 1972. He recorded with a number of other labels, including an imprint of his own–where he recorded two now-legendary albums with jazz pianist Bill Evans–but by the end of the 1970s, it was clear that his career had seen better days.

Around 1979, his son, Danny, took over Bennett's management. Although it took some doing, the younger Bennett turned his father's career around, introduced him to what was called "The MTV generation," and helped solidify the legend we now know as Tony Bennett, an artist idolized all over the world by an entirely new generation of fans and fellow contemporary artists like K.D. Lang and Lady Gaga.

At the age of 87, Tony Bennett remains warm, engaging, curious and appreciative of having the career he's had, of still being at it, and still being recognized as a groundbreaker and contemporary force in the industry. I'd be fibbing if I said that he remembered me, but by the end of our interview, it seemed obvious to him that I was a musician, "one of the cats," as it were, and he insisted that we get together after his July 26 gig at the Sands in Bethlehem, PA. I sensed that he wanted to talk, and wanted to talk about Louis Armstrong, Art Tatum, Duke Ellington, Basie, and all those whom he believes contributed to his art. Indeed, as we reached what was the "imposed" time limit of our conversation and I wanted to cut things short–a time limit I intended to respect–he said strongly, "No, that's all right, man. I'm still goin'." And he is. You've got to love him.

BK: *As an artist, you're your own toughest critic. Let's just take the past ten years—what do you think is different about your singing?*

TB: You know, it's funny. This album that I did with Dave Brubeck from 1962 [*Bennett & Brubeck: The White House Sessions, Live 1962*] that was just released, everybody's raving about it and I forgot that I actually did it. Columbia found this thing that we recorded, when President Kennedy asked us to perform on the White House Lawn. What Dave and I did together was completely spontaneous. It's getting great reviews. It's number one on Amazon.com and with Barnes and Noble. It's a complete surprise. They're calling it a great jazz album. So I listened to it and the way I was singing and, to me, I don't think I sound better, but I think I sound the same now as I did 50 years ago, which is unusual. I was able to sustain my voice and still keep it on good shape.

BK: *I think your technique, range and breath control is better now than it was in1970, when I first heard you in person.*

TB: Thank you, that's wonderful to hear. I think one of the things you learn from being a seasoned performer is what to leave out, not "how much do you put in?" You want to simplify it.

BK: *Like Count Basie.*

TB: Right. Exactly.

BK: *I've listened to the new Bennett/Brubeck CD again and again. You cats are swingin.' What's a drag is that Dave didn't get to back up more cats like you. Is there anyone through the years that you worked with—or didn't work with—that you wanted to record with? Is there another recorded discovery out there waiting to happen?*

TB: Well, I'm sure there's going to be. In fact, next week I'm going into the recording studio to do a big jazz album with Lady Gaga. She's more than good–she's actually a terrific singer–and the songs we've chosen are really beautiful examples that show how good she really sings. Marion Evans, the great arranger, is doing the swingin' charts. I think it's going to surprise everybody that she's just that good. She works hard and is so professional. She walks in and has everything memorized. She's really a very educated artist. She's knows what she's doing.

BK: *You've done quite a bit for jazz in your books and your interviews. You've let a wider audience know about the importance of Louis Armstrong, Duke Ellington and Basie. If it were not for you, there would probably be millions of people who never heard of Bill Evans. What was it about Bill Evans that got to you and made you say, "I've got to record with this guy?"*

TB: He was behind Miles Davis and became very famous that way. I remember going into clubs so many times and hearing Bill Evans and Erroll Garner. There were just a handful of people there and they were playing beautifully. It takes a long time for that kind of thing to catch on, because it's really the most honest and most intelligent music you can hear. Ralph Sharon, my accompanist of 40 years, said on a radio interview, "I'm trying to learn how to play like Bill Evans." Not only him, but every other piano player that I know of says they're trying to learn how to play like Bill Evans. Years ago, it was all about Art Tatum. Everybody wanted to play like Art Tatum. Bill Evans represents another concept and everybody wants to learn to play like Bill Evans. There's an album he made where he played J.S. Bach with a symphony orchestra. I listened to it a lot, and all of a sudden I realized that he sounded better than the whole symphony. You could hear that. He was just a genius and a wonderful person. He regretted his habit. He couldn't stand the fact that he got hooked on narcotics.

BK: *You've spoken eloquently and extensively about Duke Ellington and how important he was to you personally and professionally. But I get the sense, even after reading many of the books written about him, that not a lot of us really knew the guy. I think you did.*

TB: He was a complete genius. He never stopped writing. Every night he composed, and the next day the band would play it at a rehearsal. The band was his sketch pad. An artist uses a sketch pad to plan a painting. That orchestra was his sketch pad. He was so different from anyone and so creative. For instance, any other bandleader would hire saxophones, trumpets and trombones and a rhythm section. He would search for individual artists like Paul Gonsalves, Johnny Hodges. Everyone in the orchestra was an artist in his own right. They were completely different. Johnny Hodges just wasn't another saxophone player. He was Johnny Hodges. And the same thing with Paul Gonsalves. Everyone in the band was special. He chose artists that were individuals who knew how to make things work. And that's how Duke worked. He didn't write for a saxophone player. He wrote for Johnny Hodges. He respected all his musicians very much. He taught me to do two things. He said, "Don't do one thing, do two." I had a passion for painting and Duke turned me on to painting every day, and I've been doing that for many years. And that came from Duke Ellington, and that was important to me, because music and art share the same premise and they feed one another. What you learn when you paint, you learn about music, and what you learn from music, you learn about painting. It's funny how it worked for me. I'm very content with what I do. There's a continuity going with the two mediums that I work with, and it's a pleasure to keep learning that way. My ambition is to keep getting better as I get older, to swing it, and to prove that you don't have to give up on life just because you're getting old.

BK: *If a young person studying music today wanted to be a part of your rhythm section, what would you tell them? What do you look for in your accompanists?*

TB: I look for a jazz artist. One of the things that interviewers often ask is whether or not I get tired of singing "San Francisco" over and over again, and ask if I get tired of doing the same songs every night. With jazz artists, you never get tired of it. I have Gray Sargeant on guitar and he's phenomenal. He's a complete jazz artist, and there isn't a night that he plays the same solo. It's always completely different, and inventive. This is what I need in support. I need jazz artists. I don't like working big stadiums. I like nice acoustical halls where it's intimate. And the acoustics change from night to night and that also makes things different for all of us. It becomes a show unto itself, even though it's the same repertoire. It's different every night.

BK: *Because they're inspiring you, and that makes you sing differently every night?*

TB: Right. It makes everything like the first time you're doing it. And that's good for the audience. They feel that it's the first time something's happening and they know that the same thing isn't happening every night.

BK: *You've said Louis Armstrong was a tremendous influence on you.*

TB: Not only me, but everybody. Dizzy Gillespie said, "Without Louis, there would be no me." Everybody was inspired by him. He invented bop. He invented scat singing. The new thing is rap. You'll find out he did that, too. Whenever anything else catches on, you'll find it's something that Louis did a long time ago. He was so humorous. They asked him, "Who's your favorite vocalist?" His answer was, "You mean after Ella?" He had a wonderful sense of humor, and a great spirit about doing the right thing all the time. Classical trumpet players learned from him. They couldn't believe what he was doing and they actually changed their method of playing in terms of tonality and attack. He influenced everybody. With him, it was always the right beat and the right feeling. He makes you happy.

BK: *Like Armstrong, you'll still be talked about in the distant future. Will people also be talking about Frank Sinatra then?*

TB: Absolutely. He was my idol. He was ten years older than I was. He was a beautiful, beautiful singer. His work is very impressive to me and will always be. I always loved him so much, personally. He changed my life in many ways by just being a great friend of mine throughout my life. When he called me his favorite singer, it changed my whole career. All of his fans checked me out and I've been sold out ever since. He was a big influence on my life.

BK: *With the state of jazz today, do you think it has a future?*

TB: Yeah—but jazz has taken a back seat. For example, CBS just did four specials on country music. They're raving about the ratings, and they're saying that 65 percent of Americans love country music. And they said contemporary music is about 50 percent. And when they got to jazz, they gave it like 13 percent. You know, there's still a lot of bigotry about jazz because jazz was invented by African Americans. There still are a lot of people—especially corporate people—who think that people just don't like jazz. I think it's a silly and bigoted attitude. Because when you think of it, Fred Astaire spent his whole life singing jazz. He introduced all of the greatest songs that they call the Great American Songbook. I call it the Fred Astaire Songbook. Gershwin, Cole Porter and Irving Berlin would not make a move unless Fred Astaire introduced their songs. You could hear him syncopating and improvising throughout his whole life. All his performances had a beat to it with unexpected moves. And different each time. It was really a jazz attitude. – *ICON magazine, 2013.*

"TEEN IDOL ON THE ROCKS: A TALE OF SECOND CHANCES," BY BOBBY RYDELL

Those music fans of a certain age who pigeonhole singer Bobby Rydell as a flash-in-the-pan teen idol are obviously not aware that the entertainer was and is a world class singer, favorite of not-easy-to-please colleagues like Frank Sinatra and Buddy Rich, a fine percussionist, film and television actor, and an artist who has had long associations with jazz musicians like Pat Martino.

Born Robert Ridarelli in South Philadelphia in 1942, the entertainer later known as Bobby Rydell has had an incredible career, and has survived personal and professional setbacks that are simply astonishing. This is a man who was on television at the age of 10, had million-selling records before he was out of his teens, almost had his career ruined when the Beatles arrived in 1964, beat alcoholism, and unbelievably lived through a medical miracle when he had a dual, liver/kidney transplant.

His autobiography, *Bobby Rydell: Teen Idol on the Rocks, a Tale of Second Chances* (Doctor Licks publishing), written with help from award-winning author/filmmaker Allan (*Standing in the Shadows of Motown*) Slutsky, is chock full of brutally honest and sometimes shocking personal and professional revelations, but it is also a factual chronicle of the history of Philadelphia record labels, and rich entertainment history. The Philadelphia musical community will have a real field day reading about local legends like drummer Carl Motolla, saxophonist Georgie Young, Cameo Parkway record label mavens Bernie Lowe and Dave Appell, arranger/saxophonist Bill Zaccagni, and the rest of the gang.

Rydell is one of the very few "teen rock idols" to have successfully transitioned to performing before adult audiences. At the age of 19, he was the youngest performer ever to have starred at New York City's Copacabana. But although he continued to work, his career was never the same after The Beatles arrived. Beginning in 1985, the lean years were miraculously over for him thanks to promoter Dick Fox, who put together something called "The Golden Boys of Bandstand," starring Rydell, Fabian and Frankie Avalon. Sure, the Golden Boys were often at each other's throats, according to the author, but the unit toured successfully until Rydell's health tanked in 2012, the year he had his double transplant surgery.

This is a heck of a tale and certainly well written, and thankfully, the author is honest and open enough to answer some difficult questions about the course of his career–he could have been a major film star via his role in "Bye, Bye Birdie," released in 1963 but he elected to stay based in Philadelphia–the troubled relationship with his mother, and possible reasons for his alcoholism.

While he does admit that the 1970s until the arrival of Golden Boys were relatively lean years, more detail about just how he actually survived those years professionally and personally–names, dates, gigs, etc.–would have been welcome.

Overall this is a frank and touching tale of survival with a happy ending. As of today, Bobby Rydell is in good health, is busier than ever and is finally getting the credit he deserves as a versatile and first-class entertainer. Given Allan Slutsky's background in film and close association with this book, a Rydell biopic is certainly a possibility, and an uplifting story about a certifiable survivor–rather than films about junkie, wife-beating jazz trumpet players, would certainly be welcome. – *Backstage, 2016.*

AL MARTINO (1927-2009)

Singer Al Martino, who was one last of still-working, Italian troubadours with wide, hit-making appeal, died on October 13 at his home in suburban Philadelphia. Martino's death, at the age of 82, was a shock to his family and friends, as there was no inkling of illness. In fact, he was still working and sounding great and booked well into the next year.

At time of his death in 2009, the only living, Italian-American singers of a similar, stylistic mode who could rival Martino in terms of numbers of records sold–Martino recorded chart-toppers from the early 1950s through the 1970s–were Jimmy Roselli, then 84; Jerry Vale, then 79; and Vic Damone, then 81. In 2009, all were retired. Al Martino was not.

Born Alfred Cini in South Philadelphia, he first worked as bricklayer in his father's masonry business. Young Al loved listening to singers like Perry Como, Al Jolson, and especially his neighborhood pal, Mario Lanza. After World War II service–he was wounded in the Iwo Jima invasion–he decided on a singing career, changed his name to Al Martino, moved to New York City, and in 1948, garnered a television appearance on tremendously influential *Arthur Godfrey's Talent Scouts* television show.

As a result of his first place win on the Godfrey show, he recorded a song entitled "Here in my Heart" for a small Philadelphia record label. Despite the size of the record company, that single ultimately became a number one hit, first in England and then stateside. He signed with Capital Records in 1953. Although he had many hits through the years, including "I Love You Because," "Volare," "Spanish Eyes" and the famed "Love Theme from the Godfather" ("Speak Softly Love"), Martino's career floundered several times over the years, rumored to be a result of mob ties.

His first reported "problem," repeated in the official Martino biography, was in the mid-1950s, when his contract was said to have been taken over by a "connected" manager, and the singer was ordered to pay $75,000 in "protection" money. Martino high-tailed it to England, where he appeared regularly, but he had next to no visibility in the states until 1958, when a friend intervened on Martino's behalf. The friend, never named, must have been quite influential.

Then there was the controversy involving Martino's role as singer Johnny Fontane in all three *Godfather* films. Writer Mario Puzo's Johnny Fontane character was said to be loosely based on that of Frank Sinatra during the early 1950s period when Sinatra was down on his luck and needed a break. Old Blue Eyes got his break, according to the *Godfather* novel, with mob help. It was said that Sinatra was not thrilled with the character of Johnny Fontane. Other insiders claim the book and the films were among Sinatra's favorites.

Several non-acting singers, including Vic Damone, who was ready to take the role and actually secured Sinatra's blessing, were offered the Fontane role–even Sinatra himself was said to have been approached–but Martino ultimately got the part. It is not known for certain whether or not Martino went to Mr. S. for his "official sanction," but the singing career of Al Martino and the quality of the dates he was offered mysteriously suffered after the release of *The Godfather*. There aren't many in showbiz still around who know exactly what happened. Those who do know have nothing to say.

Al Martino

Martino again turned to overseas audiences. Until the end, he was particularly beloved in England and Germany. His final date was on October 3, at a Staten Island tribute to his boyhood friend and inspiration, Mario Lanza.

Like Jerry Vale and Jimmy Roselli, Martino received some early, classical training, though Martino's voice could be termed the most "operatic." All three, in their heyday, had substantial lung power. More importantly, they were true stylists with a passion and, yes, schmaltz, that died with Frank Sinatra.

No matter what their ethnic background, millions of listeners became misty-eyed listening to Martino sing "Here in my Heart" or Vale crooning "Al Di La" through the years. Perhaps those songs and those artists reminded all of us of a simpler and happier time.

Al Martino did that, successfully and sincerely, for six decades. – *Backstage, 2009.*

LOU RAWLS: (1933-2006)

Lou Rawls, who died today at the age of 72, was never a jazz singer, per se, though he recorded with a number of giants through the years, and helped introduce millions of people to jazz who might not have listened to it otherwise. The presumption is that if folks felt that "Lou Rawls was a jazz singer" then jazz "must be good." He opened the doors for singers and instrumentalists like George Benson and dozens of others, never misrepresented his talents, and while he did experience the hit records, "You'll Never Find" among them, I don't believe he ever subverted his talent for the sake of sales.

His work on behalf of the United Negro College Fund was legendary, and if memory serves, only Lou Rawls was able to get a certain Mr. Francis Albert Sinatra to appear on the then fledgling UNCF telethon, only a struggling syndicated operation at that point. Such was the charm and the talent of Lou Rawls.

He had almost a reassuring voice, some would say maybe an outgrowth of King Cole and Billy Eckstine, with none of the excesses that we hear–okay, I hear–of today's alleged, jazz and jazz oriented singers, male and female.

Lou Rawls, to his credit, was pretty much free from scandal and the gossip column and tabloid mongers through the years. He must be one of the few. On a personal basis, and that's the only way I'm able to measure a man accurately, I can report that Lou Rawls was quite special.

He was performing in the main room of Atlantic City's famed Golden Nugget Hotel and Casino, circa 1984. This was during the "golden age," at least entertainment-wise, of Atlantic City. It's difficult today to realize that it existed. Think of it: the main stages were populated by the likes of Frank Sinatra, Dean Martin, Don Rickles, Steve and Eydie, Vic Damone, Eddie Fisher, Diana Ross, Al Martino, George Carlin, Alan King, Shecky Greene, and yes, Lou Rawls. But the real action, for those "in the know," was in the lounges. It was unbelievable, as this "free" lounge entertainment included talents like Keely Smith, Chris Connor, Earl Hines, Teddy Wilson, Red Norvo, Buddy Greco, Billy Eckstine, Billy Daniels, Joanie Sommers, Sam Butera and The Wildest, Dakota Staton, Frankie Randall (also the Nugget's Entertainment Director) and dozens of others. Incredible.

Lou Rawls

I had a wonderful association with Atlantic City back then, both playing in the lounges with vocalists Coni Lesem and Sonny Averona, and my own combinations; as well as writing a regular entertainment column for *Atlantic City* magazine. What a time.

Around this time, I had become enamored, and there is no better word, of singer Joanie Sommers, then working the Golden Nugget lounge. Trying to make an impression and win her over, I became something of her gopher/messenger/pr person/major domo, be it carrying her music, rehearsing the band, running interference with the front office, trying to book her and get her in to the columns, etc. I had no idea of how much I was embarrassing myself.

That's when Lou Rawls stepped in. One fine evening at the conclusion of her Golden Nugget lounge show, circa 2:00 a.m., I was waiting outside the lounge with hat in hand, truly dejected, and with Joanie's music in my other hand. It appeared, literally and figuratively, that I had been left holding the proverbial bag while Ms. Big Time Lounge Singer was off to party with the big wigs. And who should appear out of thin air at that moment? Lou Rawls.

"You don't need this, kid," Lou said to me. "You're a talent in your own right; playing here, writing your column. I'm telling you not to do this. You're bringing yourself down. Get rid of her and forget it, man."

"How did you know what's going down?" I asked Lou.

"Everyone can see it," he replied, "and Frankie Randall asked me to talk to you."

Things changed a few years after that. Atlantic City has never been the same and I was never the same. It was a magic time. People cared about entertainment then. People cared about people then. Lou Rawls took the time to talk to a sad, lovesick young fellow and set him straight.

And Lou, it worked. May you rest–and keep swinging soulfully–in peace. – *Backstage, 2006.*

ANITA O'DAY: THE LIFE AND TIMES OF A JAZZ SINGER

Anita O'Day. There will never be another like her in the history of jazz. Along with Billie Holiday, Ella Fitzgerald, Sarah Vaughan, Betty Carter, and perhaps one or two others, she influenced scores of jazz singers and virtually created a language – and set the standard– for true, modern jazz singing.

Yes, she lived what used to be called the "jazz life," with a decades-long substance abuse problem, destructive relationships, and what can gently be termed as career highs and career lows. But through her astounding professional life that lasted from the early 1930s to her death at the age of 87 in 2006, she always, always performed at the highest level. As detailed in her 1981 autobiography, *High Times, Hard Times*, life was rarely easy, and she almost lost that life more than once due to addiction.

Professionally, she was a perfectionist who only demanded of her accompanists what she demanded of herself. Above all, Anita O'Day was a survivor. In the true sense of the word.

Jazz aficionados are fortunate that O'Day was amply represented on recordings, both authorized and unauthorized, from 1941 until her death, and that a good amount of performance film exists. Those films include her film shorts with Gene Krupa from the early 1940s, her memorable appearance in the legendary *Jazz on a Summer's Day* documentary about the Newport Jazz Festival from 1958. a guest stint on the Timex All-Star Jazz television show from the same year with Krupa and Lionel Hampton, a wonderful concert from Japan in 1963, a hard-hitting turn on *60 Minutes* profile from 1980, and various other odds and ends.

As incisive as her autobiography was and is (none other than Madonna was reported to have owned the rights to it for some time) along with the great recordings and videos, Anita O'Day's real story–and the impact she had and has in the world of jazz–has never really been told. Until now.

"*Anita O'Day: The Life of a Jazz Singer*" is an award-winning film, completed in 2007 and now available on DVD, that truly tells the tale of a legend. Co-directed by Robbie Cavolina and Ian McCrudden, this marvelous production includes film of Anita's interviews with Dick Cavett, David Frost, Bryant Gumble (the one with Gumbel is worth the price of admission), and comments from her fellow artists and collaborators through the years, including Buddy Bregman, Russ Garcia, Bill Holman, Johnny Mandel, Annie Ross, George Wein and Joe Wilder.

Taken as a cinematic whole, *Anita O'Day: The Life of a Jazz Singer* is Academy Award-winning material.

O'Day's first break as a singer was in 1938, when she began appearing at Chicago's Off-Beat club, where she caught the attention of Krupa. She continued working around Chicago until she joined the GK crew in 1941. Her duet with Krupa trumpeter Roy Eldridge, "Let Me Off Uptown," became a hit, and she was named "New Star of the Year" by *DownBeat* magazine. When Krupa disbanded in 1943, she briefly joined Woody Herman's band, then the orchestra of Stan Kenton, where she again hit on wax with "And Her Tears Flowed Like Wine." She rejoined Krupa in 1945 and stayed a year. Many fans of that "ace drummer man" consider his 1945 band to be his best. After that, she worked as a single.

Her contribution to the Krupa band was a substantial one (and they had a number of live and recorded reunions until Gene's death in 1973). Before her arrival in the Krupa fold in 1941, and the arrival of cohort Roy Eldridge, the band was a not-particularly-distinguished swing crew that was highlighted by a few decent soloists and more than a few drum features by the leader. When Anita and Roy came on the scene, the band caught fire–-and Gene said this many times throughout his career– and remained one of the top bands in the business until Gene gave it up in 1951.

Anita O'Day, from the landmark film of 1960, Jazz on a Summers' Day

From 1952 to 1962, in addition to touring nationwide, she recorded a series of 17 albums for Norman Granz' Verve label and its various imprints. On an artistic basis and without exception, they still stand up today as among the most remarkable recordings in jazz history. Individually and collectively, they reveal a timeless "hipness," sense of swing and overall sensitivity that will never, ever go out of style.

In the latter 1960s, O'Day recorded a well-received series of albums for a record company she owned and operated, Emily Records. It's important to remember, that aside from the efforts of Max Roach, Charles Mingus and Dizzy Gillespie in the early 1950s, Emily was among the few and among the first, "jazz artist owned and operated" record companies in the history of jazz. Tony Bennett's ill-fated "Improv" label, as well as those started by George Shearing, The World's Greatest Jazzband, and Stan Kenton, came much later.

Her final album, *Indestructible*, was recorded in 2004 and 2005, and released in 2006. It was her first recorded effort in 13 years. She died in November of 2006, seven months after its release.

The jury is still out on Robbie Cavolina, O'Day's manager for some years until her death, and truly the mastermind behind the film. He almost single-handedly ensured that O'Day got the credit she deserved as an icon and an innovator during her lifetime. That Anita O'Day was around for 87 years–and still singing–had much to do with his dedication. However, some in the industry maintain that O'Day had no business singing in public for the last several years of her life and that *Indestructible* should have never been released, in that she was way, way beyond a shadow of her former singing self. I did an appearance with her at the *Denver Jazz on Film Festival* in 2004, and can unequivocally state that she had no business being there, much less singing. Some believe Cavolina kept O'Day working purely as a cash cow. Cavolina has said that O'Day just wanted to continue singing. Whatever the case, Anita O'Day is best remembered for the work contained in this essential jazz documentary. – *Backstage, 2009.*

Postscript: Despite the awards and the accolades, "Anita O'Day: The Life of a Jazz Singer" sunk without a trace, though it is still available commercially on DVD if you look hard enough for it. Those within the company that produced it claim Robbie Cavolina played fast and loose with the money. Cavolina claims just the reverse.

FRANK SINATRA AT 100

Given that Frank Sinatra would have been 100 years old in 2015, and with the release of new books, documentary films, tribute albums and newly-discovered recordings, it seems fitting and proper to devote a 2015 *Backstage* column to an appreciation of Mr. S.

Before going into this personal back story, let it be said for the record that it is a testament to Frank Sinatra's star power that his name is still selling books for the likes of James Kaplan, who never met the man, and relied upon previously published sources that may or may not have been accurate. If Mr. S. was still here, you can bet that Mr. Kaplan and his clones would have been made offers they could not refuse.

I first saw Frank Sinatra in person in 1967 at Philadelphia's Convention Hall. My brother, a Sinatra-type singer at the time, insisted that I go and insisted that we both wear coats and ties. Also on the bill were Buddy Rich and his Orchestra and Sergio Mendes and Brazil '66. Obviously, I had heard of Sinatra, as my brother was a major fan, but I knew little about him, and being a drummer, my main interest was Buddy Rich. Rich, of course, was spectacular, and Mendes always had a pleasing group. There was an intermission, and after no announcement whatsoever, Frank Sinatra walked out on the stage. Lightning bolts of electricity went through me when this man hit the stage, and didn't even really know about him or care about him before. In my years in the entertainment business, I have never had that feeling again. Such was the power of Francis Albert Sinatra, and I probably saw him in person more than 20 times since that night.

One of the first articles I had published, shortly after graduating Temple University, was a review of a Sinatra show. From that time onward, I always made sure his office got copies of whatever it was I was putting out at the time, including newspaper articles about him, my books, videos, etc. and a strong letter of support when that brouhaha happened when the infamous Kitty Kelly book was published. He always sent me letters of appreciation, and even a color photograph inscribed in silver to me when the Kitty Kelly nonsense hit the fan.

Frank Sinatra in his heyday

Cut to 1986 and Steve Wynn's Golden Nugget Hotel and Casino in Atlantic City, now the shuttered Atlantic Club. The Nugget ended up having many of the superstar entertainers that were formally under contract to Resorts International including Frank, Dean and Sammy. The Nugget's lounge in Atlantic City was often the last stop of the evening while on my journalistic beat, and, as detailed elsewhere in these pages, was the spot where I first heard and fell for singer Joanie Sommers.

In addition to being smitten, I took on Joanie Sommers as a personal cause, and I planned on using every connection I had in the business to resuscitate her career. I got her a meeting with Vegas entertainment maven Maynard Sloate at the Sahara Hotel and Casino, and I managed to get her good representation, in the form of Andrea Kauffman, Frank Sinatra, Jr.'s agent for many years.

My ace in the hole, so I thought, was Junior's father, "Old Blue Eyes" himself. Sinatra was then affiliated with The Golden Nugget, and every lounge attraction in existence was begging to be booked in the Nugget lounge when "The Old Man" was upstairs in the main room. The idea was that maybe, just maybe, Sinatra would come into the lounge after his show to check out whoever was performing. What a possible career boost.

Joanie was doing several weeks per year at The Nugget, but my plan was to ensure that she was booked during one of Mr. S's performance, and to figure out a way to get him in the lounge to hear her.

I wrote Mr. S. a heartfelt letter about all this and not long after, I was astonished to discover that he got Entertainment Director Frankie Randall to book Joanie Sommers in the lounge during his next, headlining Nugget gig. Randall promised to see what he could do to get Sinatra in the lounge to hear Joanie. One night it happened. The private security phone behind the bar rang, alerting all appropriate parties and security that "the man" was on his way. And there he was, greeting me at the bar with a "hi, kid," and then sat with Jilly Rizzo and some members of his band, including drummer Irv Cottler and bassist Jim Hughart.

I continue to be amazed that this happened, and though nothing ever came of it for Joanie except plenty of more bookings at the Nugget and when it changed over to Bally's Grand. I vowed never to write or speak ill—in the slightest way—of Frank Sinatra. The National Enquirer, among others, knew of my writing skills and "on the scene" involvement with showbiz folk in Atlantic City. They called me at my home and offered me a substantial amount of money to give them dirt on Frank and other celebs who were passing through AC. I turned them down.

In the early 1990s, he did me another great favor. I was writing and co-producing my video documentary on Buddy Rich. There was no YouTube back then, so those of us producing documentaries had to find vintage film footage the old fashioned ways: letters and phone calls. I had recalled reading, a few years back, that the Sinatra company took back full ownership from Paramount Pictures of the famous *Concert for the Americas* show that took place in the Dominican Republic in 1982. Buddy Rich and his band appeared in that concert and BR, of course, did a fabulous drum solo, which I had hoped to use in what became the *Buddy Rich: Jazz Legend* video. Again, I went to the Sinatra office, and two weeks later, Dorothy Uhlleman, who ran the office, told me that Mr. S. wanted her to tell me the following: "Anything for the kid."

Interestingly, about three months before his death on May 14, 1998, Uhlleman called me again to ask for copies of the Buddy Rich videos, which had somehow become misplaced. "The Boss wants to watch them," she said.

My final personal encounter with Sinatra is almost impossible to adequately describe via the written word. In early 1987, the Bally Manufacturing Company purchased the Nugget and some months later—mid-fall, if memory serves—planned a gala to end all galas for the name-changing ceremony. Much of the evening's entertainment was Frankie Randall's idea. Because it was to be such a "grand night" for the new Bally's Grand, Randall wanted to line up ten pianists from area colleges playing white baby grand pianos, headlined by George Shearing, all performing individually and collectively on the Boardwalk. Frankie and I knew each other for years and was aware that I was then on the Board of Philadelphia's Combs College of Music. He asked if Combs could provide one of the pianists, and that the hotel would pay all expenses. We lined up the (now late) Combs Dean, Dr. Daryl Hopson-Byrd, to represent Combs. But the 10 grand pianos on the Boardwalk were only the opening act. Following that performance, center stage would feature Jerry Lewis, Sammy Davis, Jr. and Frank Sinatra, and the whole evening would be broadcast worldwide via closed circuit television. Frankie Randall positioned me backstage—a place I always seemed to be, hence the "Backstage" title to many of these columns—and continuously asked me if there was anything I needed. And there I was, helping Sammy Davis on and off with his coat, talking with Mr. S (and holding his drink), and conversing with Jerry Lewis. You had to be there and I couldn't really believe I was until years later when Jerry Lewis sent me a video of the evening. Sure as hell, there I am helping Sammy on with his coat before quickly running out of frame. It indeed was "a grand night."

When Frank Sinatra passed, thousands of those in and out of the entertainment community were inconsolable. We thought he would always be around and, as radio personality, recording artist and as author Jonathan Schwartz has eloquently written, there were many of us who looked toward him as a father figure.

A week after his death, I received a package in the mail. Dorothy Ulleman sent me a copy of the funeral mass program, told me in a letter that Mr. S. would have wanted me to have it, and said how much, in his last days, he enjoyed watching the videos on Buddy Rich. I don't think I stopped crying for days.

Happy Birthday, Mr. S. – *Backstage, 2015.*

FRANK SINATRA, JR. (1944-2016)

It couldn't have been easy for the kid, and on top of it, he wanted to be a singer like his father. It might have been easier if his old man's name was Smith, but the reality was, his father's name was Sinatra. As in Frank Sinatra. No, it wasn't easy for Frank Sinatra, Jr. who just left us – unexpectedly – at the age of 72 while on tour in Daytona Beach, CA.

Certainly, senior was a great influence on the young junior. He went to as many of his dad's recording sessions as he could, began studying piano, and was ultimately drafted into singing by a group of fellow high schoolers who had a band in which he played piano. Barely out of his teens, at his father's advice, he joined the Tommy Dorsey ghost band—"there's no better training for a young singer than singing with a band," his father told him—and began to achieve a good deal of national publicity as the son who was following in his father's footsteps.

His career trajectory, which was considerable, ended on December 8, 1963, when he was kidnapped at gunpoint while working a gig with the Dorsey band at Harrah's in Lake Tahoe. The kidnappers, who demanded a ransom of $240,000, were caught within days, but at trial, the defense was that Junior planned the whole thing as a way of getting publicity for his fledgling career. The jury didn't buy it and found the kidnappers guilty in record time, but Frank Sinatra Junior's career was never the same after that. Nor was Frank Sinatra Junior. His credibility and his confidence were compromised forever.

Still, he soldiered on, often playing Vegas as an opening act, sometimes leading a big band, doing television guest shots and movie cameos, recording several albums, and gigging whenever there was a gig. However, because of his passion for what he believed was music of quality, he continued to sing the songs of the great American composers while most folks were grooving to rock and roll.

Things changed in 1988, when he received a phone call from his father, who wanted his son to conduct for him. It wasn't always trouble-free for either of them, but he conducted for his dad for seven years. " It was a wonderful experience and I miss it like you can't imagine," he said.

Frank Sinatra, Jr. later in life

After his father's death in 1998, he toured–successfully–with his "Sinatra Sings Sinatra" show. "After my father died, those are the songs audiences wanted me to sing," he said.

Those very few who knew him well–Philadelphia broadcaster Sid Mark was one–knew that Junior was not a particularly happy guy. The constant comparisons to his father, the kidnapping, the records that went nowhere and the sometimes-lousy gigs made him aloof and testy. There was a change in his last years. Credit must be given to his dedicated manager, Andrea Kauffman, who facilitated sold out overseas tours, adoring audiences, and plenty of work. Interestingly, he felt a special kinship with the younger contingent of singers, from Michael Buble to Rod Stewart, who are singing the songs Frankie had been singing for 45 years. "What they're doing pleases me," he noted.

Though his untimely death didn't get a lot of press, for me and thousands of other Frank Sinatra fans all over the world, Junior was the last connection we had to the old man. Now it's over. – *Backstage, 2016.*

AN INTERVIEW WITH FRANK SINATRA, JR.

Frank Sinatra Jr. could have taken the easy way out and chosen not to sing for a living.

But comparisons to his illustrious father have never stood in the way of his passion for the music of America's finest composers and orchestrators and his quest to have it heard.

Singing the songs from the Great American Songbook and songs of Sinatra 45 years before youngsters like Harry Connick and Michael Bublé offered their takes on it, Sinatra Jr. has worked harder than most to carve out a solid career as a vocalist, bandleader, conductor, composer and actor.

No, there haven't been any hit records, television or stage shows, but he works quite a bit, even though his "Sinatra Sings Sinatra" show is an expensive one to mount.

Frank Sinatra, Jr., born in 1944, is the middle child of three and the only boy. Although Nancy was briefly in the limelight with "These Boots Are Made for Walking," and Tina did well as a film producer and managing products with the Sinatra name, the younger Sinatra is the only sibling who maintains a visible stage presence. He was married for a while, is single now. A son, Mike, from another relationship, is a student at University of California.

The music seemed to consume him from an early age.

"When I started as a kid I wanted to be a piano player and a songwriter," he told Will Haygood of the *Washington Post*. "I only became a singer by accident. I was in college, playing in a little band. The lead singer got tanked one night. A guy in the band pointed at me and said, 'You sing?' I said, 'Me? Why me?' He said, 'You're a Sinatra aren't you? Sing!'"

As for his father, he also told the Post, "He was unreachable. He was traveling, or off making some movie. When I began in this business, with Sam Donahue's band in 1963, "it was only on rare occasions when we saw each other."

That would change decades later.

It's taken years, though, for Sinatra to finally be satisfied with his work.

"I have become a better singer," he told me. "I am now so much more comfortable working. It's taken a lot of years for me to finally arrive at that attitude, vocally."

The younger Sinatra studied his father's style carefully through the years and when and if he wants to, he can sound eerily and uncannily like his dad. A good example of this can be heard on the 1996 album "As I Remember It," a heartfelt musical and spoken tribute to Frank Sinatra.

"Yes," he says a bit reluctantly, "that was a good record."

That recording and his "Sinatra Sings Sinatra" program, where he sings many of the songs made famous by his father, stand as the exceptions through the years. After his father's death, he says, "the audience wants me to sing those songs."

Frank Jr. has long had his own eclectic repertoire (some recorded for his recent Reprise release, That Face), which dates back to one of his first studio efforts, "Spice." The title song and a dark number called "Black Night" were written by the younger Sinatra.

"Nelson Riddle knew exactly what he wanted to do with the song 'Black Night,' " Sinatra explained. "On the night that was recorded, that was March 29, 1971, it was my first album with Nelson Riddle. Something very, very difficult happened. We were in the recording studio here in Los Angeles, and Sinatra came walking in, because he heard I was recording that night. He came into the studio that night and he sat there and said, 'What an arrangement!' Nelson just blew him away. It was a very exciting evening."

As hard as it may sometimes have been for the singer to carve out a niche for himself as a performer on his own terms, there have been many, many moments through the decades that he fondly remembers.

"I was the opening act in Vegas for three years for comic Phil Harris and the legendary bandleader trumpeter Harry James," said Sinatra. "Phil Harris was one of the funniest people I ever knew. He could do more with less than anyone. He was incredible, the consummate stage performer who was also one hell of a musician. He was just brilliant." (Contemporary audiences will know Harris as the voice of Baloo in the 1967 Walt Disney film, *The Jungle Book*).

A thoroughly studied musician, Sinatra continues to be fascinated by the orchestrations, many featured in the "Sinatra Sings Sinatra" program, that made the music of Frank Sinatra timeless.

How is it that those arrangements by craftsmen like Riddle, Gordon Jenkins, Billy May, Don Costa, Billy Byers and the rest sound as if they were written yesterday?

Sinatra's explanation is that "they knew how to orchestrate. They knew how to make best use of the musical instruments. They knew how to write counterpoint in music. They knew how to make the instruments sound as they wanted them to sound."

In 1988, while leading, conducting and singing with his own band at downtown Las Vegas' Four Queens Casino and Hotel, Frank Sinatra Jr. received a telephone call that would put his years of study, listening, learning and performing to the ultimate test.

"I had been conducting for myself," he explained. "And the reason why I had been doing that is because we were working on such a small stage that there was no room for a conductor. So I ended up conducting for myself. When Sinatra came in one night, he said, 'My God, the kid conducts!' In his eyes, all of a sudden I was Eugene Ormandy, you know what I mean?

"He called me in early 1988. I was in my hotel room in Atlantic City and I was discussing the show that we were doing with my trumpeter, Buddy Childers, and my drummer, Bob Chmiel. The phone rang and my father was on the phone, which surprised me, and he said to me, 'Why don't you come out and conduct for me?'

"So when my friends revived me with the smelling salts, I said, 'What in the world is going on?' He said, 'I need somebody to conduct for me.' I said, 'What's the matter with the guy you've got?' Then I had to hold the phone away because he was yelling. He said, 'These people don't have the slightest idea of what I'm doing!' Then he said to me, 'Maybe another singer would understand what a singer is trying to do.' And that was a pretty revolutionary thing to do. You never go to a show to hear a singer and see that the show is being conducted by another singer.

"He brought me in, and I began to learn him. I knew the music. I had to learn him. I was with him the last seven years that he worked. It was a wonderful experience and I miss it like you can't imagine. It was a learning experience, and it was probably the greatest compliment that he ever gave me. And he didn't give out compliments easily."

After his father's death in 1998, Frank Sinatra Jr. again hit the road with his own band. And one of the key members of the band was the pianist and sometimes conductor of his father's orchestra, Bill Miller.

Miller, best known for being the pianist on the elder Sinatra's famed "One for My Baby" was the original lounge pianist at the Desert Inn in Las Vegas in 1951.

"My father was playing at the Desert Inn that year," Sinatra recalled, "and I believe it was the first year that he ever played Las Vegas. "He met Bill Miller and loved his touch and the way he played. Bill Miller joined Sinatra in 1951. In 1951, I was seven. Bill would come to our home and rehearse with my father. I was taking piano lessons already, but I listened to a professional, and I tried to get the touch on the piano that Bill Miller had.

"As the years went by, whenever there was a Sinatra recording session and I could go to it, I would make it my business to be there and listen to the arrangements. But I would always find myself standing by the piano, listening to what Bill Miller was doing. Without knowing it, he was my teacher.

"Bill was with my father for almost 45 years. After my father died, Bill had been in retirement. In October of 1998, I went to Atlantic City to work and I was surprised to learn that the hotel who had booked us was the final hotel Sinatra performed in when he was still working. So I got an idea in my head.

"I told my people I wanted the big orchestra and that I was going to call Bill Miller to see I could convince him to come out of retirement. Bill Miller came to Atlantic City, and with very low, ethereal music playing, he was sneaked onto the stage and started to play his famous 'One More For my Baby.' And when the lights came up on him, people recognized him and they gasped.

"I was sitting there in the darkness, and the older I get, the more I look like Sinatra. When I was sitting there in a dark blue light, in my tuxedo, the resemblance was a little striking. The people were dead silent, and it really moved them, so much so, that they had tears in their eyes. Bill Miller worked with me until July, 2006, when he had a heart attack and died. He played right up until the end. His daughter came up to me after his death, telling me, 'You gave my father another eight years of life.' But Bill died never knowing what he taught me about music. I miss him every day."

Of the new breed of singers who have followed in his father's footsteps, Sinatra is "just glad they're doing better music. That also goes for Rod Stewart and Michael Bolton, who are both friends of mine. The fact that they're singing better music pleases me a great deal. They're going to educate a generation."

As for the future, Sinatra will continue to take work, when the gig is right, with nothing less than a full orchestra, playing the great songs and the great arrangements. There may be more film and television roles down the line per his guest spots on *The Sopranos*, and he has just completed a second appearance on *The Family Guy.*

Musically? In a 2001 essay entitled "Frank Sinatra is Alive and Well and Singing in Europe," poet and Sinatra family friend Rod McKuen, hit the nail on the head when he commented, "Frank Sinatra Jr. is his own man, and while he's proud to be 'the keeper of the flame' at this point in time, there is absolutely no doubt that he will be creating his own standards as a singer and writer in the near, not distant, future." Or, as no less than the *Washington Post* put it in 2006, Frank Sinatra Jr. is "uniquely gifted in his own right." – *Naples (FL)Daily News, 2008.*

AN INTERVIEW WITH HARRY CONNICK, JR.

As a performer, there just isn't much that Harry Connick Jr. hasn't done. He's conquered almost every existing medium and has done a good deal of what he does without compromise and with integrity intact.

And other than Gene Krupa, he is the only "matinee idol"–if there still are such things–ever produced by the world of jazz.

Since first breaking through as a jazz pianist when he signed with Columbia Records in 1988, he has reached an incredible level of fame as a concert attraction, star of Broadway, television and motion pictures; recording artist, jazz pianist, vocalist, and as used to be said, star of stage, screen and television. He has carried this considerable fame with modesty, dignity, confidence, grace, humility, sincerity, passion, good humor and a dedication to his craft and to his first love, jazz.

All of this came through during a recent and wide-ranging conversation that covered everything from "talking technical shop," to the future of jazz, to his present, past and future in the business.

By his own admission, he is an intensely private person and consequently, to his credit, may be the first mega-star in history to not have become tabloid fodder. Until 2013 that is, by way of a "situation" played out on national television, on *American Idol*, no less, one of the most-watched television programs in the country.

For those who missed it, Connick was a "guest mentor" on the program, meaning that his role was to give advice to some of the up-and-comers. The timing of his appearance was appropriate, as in that episode, the singing competitors were asked to perform an American pop song classic. Among the songs sung were "My Funny Valentine" and "Stormy Weather." Connick was, shall we say, a bit hard on the contestants and their "renditions," strongly pointing out that a singer must know what the song is about before it is sung. The guest mentor made it quite clear that, from what he h eard, it was obvious they had no idea.

The next day, the national jazz community went wild on social media, saying in part that it was about time someone said this. And that Harry Connick Jr. was the man to say it.

"I didn't plan on saying what I said," he remembers, "and I had no idea the jazz community was so happy about what I said. What I did hear was that I got in a fight with [judge] Randy Jackson, and I think that's hysterical. First, it wasn't a fight. Talking like this stimulates people and that's what we love to do: talk about music. The last I checked, that show is about music. I like Randy Jackson. I've known him for years. I just disagreed with him. With the whole mentoring thing, what I believe is that there are a couple of ways to learn how to play. You listen to records, you go out on gigs, and whenever you have an opportunity to learn from the older cats, you do. In this case, I was the older cat and was teaching them what I thought would help them. But what they didn't show was the half-hour that I spent with each of them, when I said, 'Take this stuff with a grain of salt. This is what I think, but you all have to do what you have to do. Which I think they all ended up doing anyway.

"Right after I did that, I called my mentor and teacher Ellis Marsalis on the phone and said 'thanks.' I'd be playing a tune in his class, and he would ask, 'What are the lyrics?' I'd be playing it, and not singing it, but he still wanted me to know what the lyrics were. He would say, 'What's the tune about?' I would say, 'I don't know' and then he would say, 'Well, then you can't play it. You need to learn the lyrics. You need to know what you're playing about. And that goes for the verses, too.' He was brutal with us. That's how you learn.

"What you also didn't see on the air was that I was trying to explain to them that you can't sing 'runs' unless you know harmonically what you're 'running' over. So a lot of these young women just didn't know harmony. I wasn't trying to squelch their individuality, but you can't do what they were doing unless they knew exactly what chords were going on underneath them. But it was fun and I had a good time. No, we haven't talked about me coming back, but I'd do it–mentoring–on TV or off TV."

What about today's crop of Connick wannabes?

"You know, I really don't listen," he says. "If there were a clone of me, I would be so happy, but that would mean they would have to do what I do. And I haven't seen anybody do that yet. I've seen people singing tunes, but I haven't seen those people doing the orchestrations and conducting. I haven't seen anybody present the music the way I present it. Not that I'm better than anyone else. Just because somebody sings a standard doesn't mean I'm going to stop in my tracks and check it out. This isn't a slight to any of the people out there. I honestly just don't listen."

"Passion" is one thing that comes through when speaking with him, and for him, this passion for music began in his native New Orleans when he first started taking piano lessons at the age of three. Two years later, he made his first public appearance and five years after that made his first jazz record. He fell under the spell of the elder Marsalis when he attended the New Orleans Center for Creative Arts. What has happened in his career–helped in no small measure to his marvelous soundtrack to the 1989 film, *When Harry Met Sally*–is unparalleled in show business history. When and if a history book about such things is written, it will say that only Mel Tormé almost came close to Connick's utter completeness.

Now 46, he is again tackling new territory–and a sensitive territory it is, with the making of his new CD, Every Man Should Know. This stands as the first album of all-original Connick songs, and the first ever he has written that tell of the real man, his emotions and his vulnerabilities. And he does it with a stellar group of songs that explore almost every style of music there is, including jazz, Latin, country, gospel and funk. It is impossible not to hear how deeply he is feeling about what he is singing. If Sinatra wrote songs, they might have sounded like a few of these.

Why is he opening up now? At this point in the interview Connick took a rather personal and introspective detour:

BK: *This is the first time you've let your inhibitions down and allowed the vulnerability to show and share personal experiences. Let me tell you, it really comes across.*

HC: "Wow, thank you. That means so much, man."

BK: *What possessed you to do this now?*

HC: "Like when I go in the studio–you ever see those photographs of Frank Sinatra in the studio and all these celebrities are there–I never did that. I don't feel comfortable with a bunch of people standing around. It's so focused...when I've written the orchestrations and arrangements and I go to conduct, I have to focus. I don't want to be distracted. I don't want cameras in there, I don't want people in there; so I go in the studio and I mix it and there's nobody there. It's just me and my friend Tracy and the engineer.

"I've been in this bubble and my wife tells me all the time, 'Why don't you ever let people in? Like nobody knows what you do.' I said, 'Because that doesn't matter,' and she said, 'No it does matter. Harry, I'm frustrated because I know what you can do, but nobody gets to see it.' My record company said I should open a Twitter account, something I have no interest in. And I asked my wife, 'What do you think?' and she said, 'Yeah, let people into your life a little bit.' So, today–so weird that we're talking today–I posted a video of myself in the studio– *today*!–and my wife said, 'You need to do more of that, let people into your world.'"

BK: *You got a nice lady there.*

HC: "Oh, she's great, man. And I realized how can people know what I'm doing if I don't let them into the process. I've always made up stories with my songwriting–I found it to be more fertile ground because there were no limits on what I could make up. But on *this* record, when you deal with personal experiences, it has a tendency to pull the boundaries way in. I started from that point with the lyrics and then sometimes they stayed right in the wheelhouse, but on the third track called 'I Love Her,' a bossa nova tune–that's just straight up about my wife. And then there's another song called 'Come See About Me,' which is me thinking about what it would be like not to have my wife. I never wanted to let anyone in my life before."

BK: *How does it feel? Does it take a load off?*

HC: "I don't know, man. Again, it's been a very personal process. Like on that one song, 'Come See About Me,' I started to cry because, you know, something clicked in my head when I was singing the lyrics, which is something you want to do...and I looked over at my buddy Tracy and he's like, 'Man, maybe you should do it again,' because, you know, there's nothing more heartbreaking than watching someone try not to cry. So I did it again and I really struggled and I'm wondering, man, when I go on the road–as an actor, when you're singing someone else's lyrics or something that doesn't apply to you, you can get very close to those emotions. But when they're your personal experiences...I don't know how I'm going to get through some of these tunes."

BK: *In the song* "Come See About Me," *isn't there something about "I'll pay your cab fare and letting the meter run?"*

HC: "Yeah, how pathetic. The first line of the tune is 'I don't want to bother you' and the next line he says, 'But can you come over?'"

BK: *I'm sure you'll feel it, the intensity, but as time goes on...*

HC: "Yeah, you'd think so. But I'm just wondering how I'll get through the first ten times. I was talking with Branford [Marsalis] the other day and I asked him, 'You ever cry when you play?' He said, 'Yeah,' and I asked, 'Is it hard?' And he said there's a technique to it–'I've cried when I'm playing and I've learned how to develop that sound and use it when I want to use it if I can't access those emotions.' When you're singing, though, it's almost impossible. When you're playing the piano you can cry all you want. He said, 'Why do you ask?' and I said, 'Man, some of these songs hurt.' I think as you get older you realize life's too short and you start letting the silly stuff go and you cut down to the common denominator of who you are–and that's pretty scary, because you start cryin' about stuff."

BK: *I'm hearing things in your voice—there's emotion here, it's heavy. They're beautifully written tunes, but it's how you sound on them, which is what you're saying to me.*

HC: "I really want to go in the studio and do a record that's all ballads, kind of under the umbrella of [Frank Sinatra's album] Only the Lonely. It's just ballad after ballad of, you know, sad songs. I would like to see how I'd sound on that, because I'm definitely able to access different emotions now. Sometimes if you start letting that stuff go, other kinds of performances come out."

BK: *I'm just curious—was there ever a time when you were a musical snob? I mean, today if it ain't* "Night in Tunisia,*" forget about it.*

HC: "Oh, man, I'm so glad you asked about that. That's another thing that Branford and I were talking about. We all were under the Wynton [Marsalis] spell, and I don't think even Wynton's under the Wynton spell anymore. If it wasn't clean, it was blasphemy. I would have never put a tune like the first one ['What Every Man Should Know'] on this record. I mean, there's no way. I would never have even used an electric bass. I still have a problem with keyboards. But those were the years that it was about honing my craft. I couldn't hone my craft unless I spent all my waking hours working on it. What I didn't realize in that snob phase was I forgot about my history. When I was 18 I got signed to do a jazz record and I stopped playing classical, stopped playing rock. And then a few years down the road I made a couple of New Orleans funk records and then people looked at me as though I was from Mars. And that was about the time that I said, screw it, you know, who am I answering to? I know the rules, I know how to play, why can't I play what I want to play? So this record is a testament to that. The tunes kind of wrote themselves. It's like the old Michaelangelo story when they asked him how he carved the horse out of a block of marble, he said 'I just chipped away everything that wasn't a horse.'"

Harry Connick, Jr.

The only critical barbs he's endured through the years, however mild they were, came from that group of self-righteous musical purists who were not thrilled about his forays into funk or anything else that didn't have to do with jazz.

"Hey, I was playing with the funk band, The Meters, when I was growing up, and was playing rock and roll gigs. But when I got to New York and signed with Columbia, I stopped doing everything but jazz. So this new project is a testament to that."

Regarding the future, he's open to almost anything, including writing something he describes as a "long form, symphonic, symphonic type thing," but his plans definitely do not include conducting any Pops orchestras, Philly Pops or otherwise. "It just wouldn't do much for me," he says. "I spend so much time conducting my own stuff."

"No rules, no limits," is how Connick describes the songs on his new CD, but that description it also applies to the artist, to the man and his music. Indeed, there was a song once sung by one of Connick's influences, that may sum up the life and art of Harry Connick, Jr. best. The name of the song is "My Way." – *ICON magazine, 2013.*

III
Now You Has Jazz

PLAYING WITH CHARLIE VENTURA

When I first took up the drums, Krupa was all I knew. While I'd like to think my drumming has advanced beyond the Krupa style, his sound, aura and charismatic personality has never left my heart. I've written two books on Gene, produced two Krupa tribute DVDs, produced several Krupa CDs, and run the jazzlegends.com web site devoted to all things GK.

As a youngster still pounding on a practice pad, my parents bought me double-LP Krupa album called *Drummin' Man*. There were two tracks on that record performed by what was called The Gene Krupa Jazz Trio, "Dark Eyes" and "Body and Soul, recorded March 8, 1945 and featuring the piano of Teddy Napoleon and the tenor saxophone of Charlie Ventura.

I hadn't heard Ventura prior to this.

I was captivated by his sound and style and by the Trio. I've never heard anything like it before or since. Was it tasteful? Was it art? Probably not, but to me, it had a passion, strength and even a schmaltz that remains unrivaled. I began looking into Charlie's life, music and career. Born in South Philadelphia, 1609 Porter Street to be exact, he became a star with Krupa, but starting in the late 1940s, he led a series of extraordinary small bands, with the moniker of "Bop for the People," designed to bring modern jazz to the masses. He won all the awards and the polls, and as late as 1957, tied with none other than Stan Getz as the nation's number one tenor in the *Playboy* magazine "Jazz Poll." He certainly advanced stylistically since those sides were made in 1945–and eventually played on bass, baritone, alto and soprano saxophones in addition to his tenor–and gave a lot of promising youngsters their start. Some of those youngsters included the singing/playing duo of Jackie Cain and Roy Kral, future Tonight Show drummer Ed Shaughnessy trombonist Bennie Green, trumpeter Conte Condoli, bassist Richard Davis, and none other than fellow Philadelphian Eddie Fisher. Ventura was forced to fire Fisher after less than a month, saying that the fledgling singer "couldn't keep time."

A young author with saxophone legend Charlie Ventura

All I knew was this: After hearing Ventura on a recording, I knew that I wanted, I needed to play drums with him, and I vowed that somehow, before I died and/or before he died, I would.

In the mid-1970s, the great Philadelphia radio and television personality, Jerry ("The Geator with the Heater") Blavat was hosting a Mike Douglas-like talk show emanating from WCAU-TV in Philadelphia. One afternoon after a day of learning and sneaking smokes at Lower Merion High School, I tuned in Blavat's show. Among the guests that day was an older gentleman who was strumming a guitar while seated on the panel with other guests. I couldn't believe it. It was Charlie Ventura himself, later joined by his vastly underrated, saxophone playing son, Charlie, Jr., for a couple of rousing tunes. He was accompanied by his long-time cohorts, Count Lewis, a.k.a. Lewis A DePasquale, on organ, and the great drum stylist, Tony DeNicola. The thing was, Charlie was in town. His home town. I had to get over to WCAU.

Having no car at my disposal, I rode my bike over to the television station and cornered Charlie just after the broadcast ended. I told him that he was my idol, and asked if he was appearing in the area. He mentioned that he was playing at a well-known restaurant and bar in center city Philadelphia, The Saxony East, later the Brass Rail, and for many years, an Italian restaurant called Portifino. It's now something called Cibo and is not doing particularly well. Charlie invited me to stop by anytime.

I must have gone into The Saxony East, sometimes alone and sometimes with friends, every night for months and months. The owners, who I came to know personally years later, took pity on me, realizing that I had next to no money, and fed me plenty of spaghetti and good Italian bread, gratis, to keep me going. I got to know Charlie, Tony and The Count quite well and continuously peppered them with questions every night. "Did you really know Charlie Parker?" "What was he like?" "Did you really know Dizzy Gillespie?" You get the idea.

They were patient and kind to this inquisitive, read: annoying, youngster. Through it all, I begged to sit in on just one tune on drums. It didn't happen. Maybe they sensed I wasn't ready.

It was obvious that Charlie had an alcohol problem. He just couldn't hold it, and after a beer or two, would become rambling and incoherent. He once introduced me to his one-time colleague, pianist John Bunch--who stopped in to visit after his gig conducting for Tony Bennett at the Latin Casino nightclub--a dozen times in the course of two minutes. I was told years later, that CV caused more than one public scene, and heard stories that he was kicked out of Las Vegas, where he lived and worked for years, under veiled circumstances. I did witness strange behavior on occasion—he threw me out of a club once as I moved his horn in order to set up my drums--but the juice never seemed to effect his playing.

One weekday afternoon, after returning home from school, my mother informed me that a "Count Lewis" had called me, and that I was to return the call asap. The phone number was that of Charlie Ventura. Charlie informed me that his drummer, Tony DeNicola, had been in a car accident, and that he needed a drummer to play several nights at The Saxony East, beginning that night. Keep in mind that he never, ever heard me play, but I guess he thought I was ready. The only musical direction he gave me was this: "Stay with the brushes until I get heavy," Charlie said. "Then pick up the sticks."

This master saxophonist was still a relatively big name at this date, especially in his native Philadelphia. He had run a popular night spot in Lindenwold, NJ, for years, called "Charlie Ventura's Open House," and was still fondly remembered. My pending gig proved to be something of an event within our family. I don't know how my mother pulled it together on such short notice, but by the time I was ready to play that night, a good dozen or so family members were seated ringside. I was a bit shaky for the first few sets and was dragging the beat, but ultimately, I caught on. I couldn't believe I was playing with my idol, the man I first heard playing "Dark Eyes" and "Body and

Soul" as a child. Man, I was Gene Krupa! Charlie was wonderful and supportive as was Count Lewis. I wish every young musician had mentors like that today. His only advice to me was that "rushing the beat a little is okay, but dragging isn't."

On a break, Charlie went over to the table to meet my folks. He asked my mother and father what nationality they were, and when they answered "Jewish," Charlie Ventura conversed with them in fluent Yiddish for a good six minutes. I was amazed. After the gig, I asked him how he did that. He said to me, "I could have done five minutes in Polish, too. When you own a nightclub, it's something you have to learn to do."

Stories about Charlie Ventura are legion. One of the funniest was told to me by Count Lewis. One Sunday afternoon, Count and Charlie were relaxing at Tony DeNicola's home in Trenton, NJ, watching the Jackie Gleason golf tournament on television. An announcement was made that comic Gleason would be playing host to President Gerald Ford on the golf course much later in the day. Hearing that, Charlie got agitated, saying, over and over again, that Gleason owed him "thousands of dollars worth of money" from a series of "mood music" records Charlie made with Gleason years ago.

Taking matters into his own hands, Charlie got on the telephone and rang up The White House, hoping to speak to The President about getting his money from Gleason. Charlie was somewhat disoriented at that point, and whoever was speaking to Charlie from The White House probably thought this was a potentially dangerous guy. According to Count Lewis, the next thing everyone knew, the DeNicola home was surrounded by a dozen Secret Service agents, who were looking for this nut case. That was Charlie for you.

Charlie Ventura moved around a lot and had some good years after leaving Philadelphia. I saw him in what was to be his last reunion with Gene Krupa at a club called Brandi's Wharf in 1971. He played a critically acclaimed series of shows with legendary pianist Teddy Wilson at Michael's Pub in New York City. Then he moved to the Sheraton Tobacco Valley in Windsor, CT, where he led a marvelous small band, and often featured guest stars like trumpeter Bobby Hackett. After some time in Denver with guitarist Johnny Smith, he ended up on the west coast, where he really cleaned up his act, but health complications–with severe dental problems on top of it–began to catch up with him. He died in the Atlantic City home of Count Lewis, who had become his caretaker, in 1992.

I've done a lot of things and met a lot of people in a career in music that has lasted almost six decades. Playing with Charlie Ventura was the highlight. – *ICON magazine, 2012.*

Gene Krupa and Charlie Ventura, possibly at Chicago's London House, 1963

"CHAMPIONSHIP JAZZ": THE FIRST–AND MAYBE ONLY–JAZZ REALITY SHOW ON TELEVISION

Television reality shows, specifically amateur talent competitions, focus on everything from singing and dancing to cooking and home remodeling. Think there will ever be a reality/competition program devoted to jazz?

You never know, but the fact is, there actually was one, and it had all the qualities of today's programming, excep that this one was anything but an amateur show. And it was never on television.

Around 1962, a jazz fan by the name of Robert Rothafel, who had served in the production department of Universal Pictures for years, had an idea for a television pilot. His concept was simple: Pit two, "name" jazz groups against each other in friendly competition, hire celebrity judges and a celebrity host, determine the winner by the amount of audience applause, award the winner $6,000 in cash and the opportunity to slug it out against another group the following week, and give the loser a generous $4,000.

This actually happened. The title was *Championship Jazz* and the television pilot was filmed before a live audience in 1962. Voice of America's famed Willis Conover was hired as host. Writer George T. Simon and Woody Herman signed on as celeb judges. The bands? The Dukes of Dixieland, and none other than the Gene Krupa Jazz Quartet featuring Charlie Ventura.

This is an absolutely incredible program and is the only filmed record of Gene's famed group at the time, which also featured pianist John Bunch and bassist Knobby Totah, playing "Drum Boogie," "Dark Eyes" and "Big Noise from Winnetka."

I won't divulge the winner.

As great as this was, it never aired and that's sad, because groups being considered as future competitors included the Modern Jazz Quartet, Oscar Peterson Trio, George Shearing Quintet, etc.

Wow! *Championship Jazz*, in the end, was ahead of its time. This is, after all, reality, but those interested in viewing this swinging program can access some of it on youtube or jazzlegends.com – *Backstage, 2010.*

GUNTHER SCHULLER (1925-2015)

Gunther Schuller – the Pulitzer Prize-winning composer, conductor, educator, French horn player, author, and longtime advocate of the co-existence of jazz and classical music – has died at the age of 89. His legacy was extraordinary and serves as a model of what could be in terms of musical acceptance, unification, cooperation, and, in the best sense of the word, fusion.

Gunther Schuller conducting the Boston Symphony.
Photo courtesy of the Boston Symphony

This was a 16-year-old French horn player who dropped out of college in 1936, performed Shostakovich's *Seventh Symphony* under Toscanini in that work's first radio broadcast, and, 14 years later, played French horn on jazz great Miles Davis's ground-breaking *Birth of the Cool* sessions.

Though he was appointed as principal French horn player with the Cincinnati Symphony Orchestra, and later served with the Metropolitan Opera Orchestra until 1959, his heart, or a good portion of it, was in jazz.

In 1955, he teamed up with John Lewis, the pianist and musical director of the Modern Jazz Quartet, to form the Modern Jazz Society, which was devoted to promoting the validity of the still-controversial Third Stream, the combination of classical music and jazz. There were those who believed in it, including Bill Evans, Ornette Coleman, and Leonard Bernstein. Others, though, like Gene Krupa, felt fusion could not work unless "the long-hairs learned how to blow hot music."

Still, Schuller's Third Stream compositions – like 1957's "Transformation" for jazz ensemble, 1950's "Concertino" for jazz quartet and orchestra, and 1960's "Variants on a Theme of Thelonious Monk" – make a good case for the validity of the Third Stream.

Though he was president of the New England Conservatory in the 1960s and 1970s and a prolific composer of classical works – "partial to the 12-tone methods of the Second Viennese School," said *New York Times* classical music writer Allan Kozinn – he somehow found time to write two important contributions to literature about jazz. In *Early Jazz*, Schuller was the first to accurately appraise the contributions of everyone from the Original Dixieland Jazz Band to Louis Armstrong, although his thoughts about Armstrong's later work did inspire some controversy. In *The Swing Era*, he gave long overdue credit to Fletcher Henderson, Basie, Ellington, Don Redman, and Woody Herman – and even made good cases for Krupa, Charlie Barnet, Glenn Miller, and Larry Clinton. Sadly, the promised follow-up will never appear.

Schuller believed that every genre could be combined with jazz or classical music, including the music of Frank Zappa and beyond. As he told *The Guardian* in 2010, "The thing that may make me unique is that I have simultaneously had seven full-time careers in music over the last 50 or 60 years. That's more than Leonard Bernstein."
– *Broad Street Review, 2015.*

B.B. KING (1925-2015)

It was 1968, and the venue was the original Electric Factory in Center City Philadelphia, the concert hall/rock club that was ultimately shut down by then-Philadelphia Mayor Frank Rizzo. Mayor Rizzo, bless his soul, never really took to "hippies." The headliner that night was the Steve Miller Band. The Factory, to its credit, always had an opening act, and though my young friends and I who were at the Factory that night considered ourselves to be students of jazz, progressive rock, and the blues, we had never heard of that night's opening attraction.

His name was B.B. King.

King didn't come out right away. Given his roots in showmanship, even the opening act had an opening act, and he was preceded by an eight-piece band, five horns and a three-piece rhythm section, who proceeded to blow all the would-be jazzers, rockers, and wannabe hipsters in attendance away with their swinging mixture of jump blues and swing. By the time the "opening act headliner" was announced, as, of course, "The King of The Blues," the audience was sufficiently pumped to go crazy when B.B. King, live and in person, walked out on stage.

B.B. King

He was already a veteran of the "chitlin' circuit," the chain of black clubs that booked him for years, when he started getting booked in rock joints like the Factory. But he did not change his act, his attitude, his musicianship, his work ethic, or his musical integrity to compensate for changing times. And those, perhaps, were the reasons why he reached, emotionally and otherwise, young audiences who had never heard of him. Hearing B.B. King play his beloved Lucille (a black Gibson ES-355 guitar) made believers out of everyone, regardless of age. Like Sinatra, B.B. King made it seem like he was singing and playing to you. His gift was that he made you *feel.*

The late 1960s was a musical era where, it seemed, all genres came together. Bands like Earth Opera; Lighthouse; Chicago; Blood, Sweat & Tears; The Mothers of Invention; Canned Heat; and Spirit, as well as those led by the likes of Steve Miller, Paul Butterfield, and Jimi Hendrix, effectively combined elements of rock, jazz, and blues to make irresistible music. Local bands like Elizabeth, Woody's Truck Stop, Sweet Stavin' Chain, and Mandrake Memorial did as well

But the real importance of this musical revolution was that it opened the door for new and revived careers – and enthusiastic new audiences – for blues veterans like Muddy Waters, Howlin' Wolf, Bo Diddley, and B.B. King. Ultimately, King was the most successful of them all, having worked 300-plus dates per year until his final performance in October of last year.

He was a major influence both on those who knew his work from his early playing (he started playing professionally in the mid-1940s) and those who didn't discover him till his 1960s "rediscovery." Shortly after his death, Eric Clapton called him a beacon; fellow blues guitarist Buddy Guy said, "The way B.B. did it was the way we all do it now." Even President Obama checked in, saying, "The blues has lost its King, and America has lost a legend. No one worked harder than B.B."

As a person, B.B. King was a showbiz rarity: someone you never heard a negative word about. Hudson Music's Rob Wallis, who produced a groundbreaking series of instructional music videos with King in the early 1990s and knew him intimately, could only say, "He was the most humble, gracious, and warm gentleman you could imagine."

That humility, grace, and warmth can all be heard in the playing and singing of B.B. King. – *Broad Street Review, 2015.*

PHIL WOODS (1931-2015)

Alto saxophonist Phil Woods, keeper of the bebop flame and one of the last surviving descendants of the Charlie "Yardbird" Parker school of playing, has died at the age of 83. He played his last job, a performance of material from famed "Charlie Parker with Strings" recordings, in Pittsburgh in early September, where he announced his retirement from playing.

In a remarkable without-compromise career that spanned six decades, he was nominated for seven Grammy Awards, winning four; was awarded the Jazz Master award from the National Endowment for the Arts; and managed to reach the non-jazz audience with his memorable solo on Billy Joel's "Just the Way You Are."

There wasn't a jazz giant Woods didn't work with. Over the years he worked with everyone from Buddy Rich and Quincy Jones to Dizzy Gillespie and Billie Holiday, but since 1974 he was best known as a leader of a quartet that often included drummer Bill Goodwin, bassist Steve Gilmore, and more recently, pianist Jim McNeely.

Like fellow alto saxophonists Cannonball Adderley, Sonny Criss, and Sonny Stitt, Woods fell under the spell of Charlie Parker early on, during his four years of study at Juilliard, where he graduated in 1952 with a major in clarinet and minor in composition. Upon the release of his first recordings in 1954, he was hailed as "The New Bird." Interestingly, a similar catchphrase was used to describe Cannonball when he first hit the scene the following year.

But Woods was much more than a Parker imitator. A technical marvel and a hard swinger at heart, he combined intellect with an individual sense of humor and tremendous versatility, continuing to evolve stylistically until the end. He had no hesitation in playing with singers and instrumentalists from all schools of jazz, from traditional to avant garde, without losing his identity. That doesn't often happen in jazz – at least not successfully.

Phil Woods was heavily involved in jazz education – he mentored Richie Cole, just to name one – and did everything he could to bring his music to as wide an audience as possible, even if it meant taking a chance.

In 1979, I was hired by the legendary Bryn Mawr folk club and coffeehouse, The Main Point, to do booking and publicity. By then, the Point had seen better days. The club couldn't compete with clubs with liquor licenses like the Bijou Café, and the few folk artists who could draw crowds were, by then, not affordable. In the Point's heyday in the 1960s, the club had some success with jazz acts, so I suggested we try that.

Phil Woods

Phil Woods had a name among general audiences since "Just the Way You Are" had just won a Grammy, so I was pretty sure he would do well for us, and in the process, perhaps open the door for other jazz bookings. I called him at his home in the Water Gap, asked if the quartet had an open weekend down the line, emphasized that the Main Point was mainly known as a folk club, and asked him for a break on money, at least the first time out.

He was gung ho and brought the group down to Bryn Mawr about a month later. He sold out four shows that weekend, was the subject of much local press, and did indeed open the door to a slew of national and regional jazz bookings at the venerable Main Point.

I've always believed that only a guy like Phil Woods could do that. He will be missed. – *Broad Street Review, 2015.*

CHUCK BERRY (1926-2017)

Chuck Berry, one of the last surviving pioneers of rock and roll, has left the building at the age of 90.

Chuck Berry at the height of his hit-making years

Berry was different from his contemporaries like Jerry Lee Lewis, Bill Haley, Little Richard and Bo Diddley. There was a calculated seriousness behind his 1950s compositions like "Roll Over Beethoven," "Sweet Little Sixteen" and "Maybelline," which were songs that generations of rockers after him–including The Beatles, The Rolling Stones, The Beach Boys and The Who–would deem as "poetry." In his interviews in later years, Berry explained that he wanted to speak to issues that were important to teens of the day: Money, romance, and in general, "teenage wishes fulfilled and good times," said Jon Pareles of *The New York Times*. And from 1954 to 1958, the hits kept on coming.

Berry was really rock and roll's first serious instrumentalist. While Haley, Jerry Lee, Diddley and even Elvis did little more than "bang it out" on the guitar, Berry listened carefully to the old blues greats, and by his own admission, jazz guitar ground-breaker Charlie Christian. Indeed, on a 1976 recording with the Steve Miller Band–*Live at the Filmore*–Berry plays a more than credible version of the jazz standard "Flyin' Home," a Benny Goodman song often played by Christian.

Unlike many old time rockers who eked out a living as oldies acts after the arrival of The Beatles, Berry continue to thrive, helped in no small measure by the public respect shown to him by members of the British invasion. "When

I hear rock, good rock, the caliber of Chuck Berry, I just fall apart and I have no other interest in life. The world could be ending if rock 'n' roll is playing," said John Lennon. The Beatles paid Chuck Berry the ultimate homage by not only recording his "Roll Over Beethoven," but via performing any number of Chuck Berry songs in live performance. Aaron Krerowicz, who bills himself as a "professional Beatles scholar," noted that The Beatles regularly performed at least 15 Berry compositions in live concerts through 1966.

Berry's personal life was checkered and in later years, despite his fame, his behavior was quirky, and in some cases, infamous. He was jailed twice, one in 1959 for "transporting a teenage girl across state lines for immoral purposes," and again in 1979 for tax evasion. It couldn't have been easy for a black man who played a music that many in white America perceived as contributing to–if not causing–juvenile delinquency. Things like that, the record company rip-offs, short royalty checks, and out-and-out thievery–Berry won a lawsuit filed against The Beach Boys for ripping off his "Sweet Little Sixteen" and turning it into "Surfin' USA" –led him to believe that showbiz was nothing more than a hustle, and he conducted himself accordingly.

More often than not, he showed up at a concert performance at the last possible minute, refused to go on stage unless he was paid in cash, and played with local pick-up bands who barely knew his songs. No matter. Audiences loved him, as did fellow rockers, including a fellow named Bruce Springsteen, who said, "Chuck Berry was rock's greatest practitioner, guitarist and the greatest pure rock 'n' roll writer who ever lived."

Not long before his death, Chuck Berry completed work on his first new recording in 38 years, comprised of all original songs. Reviews have been excellent. "This record is dedicated to my beloved Toddy," said Berry a few months before his passing, referring to his wife of 68 years, Themetta Berry. "My darlin' I'm growing old! I've worked on this record for a long time. Now I can hang up my shoes!" – *Backstage, 2017.*

"TIME REMEMBERED: THE LIFE AND TIMES OF BILL EVANS."

Classic Bill Evans

The point can be argued, but it can be said with a good deal of accuracy that the late jazz pianist and composer Bill Evans remains one of the most influential jazz pianists who ever lived, 37 years after his tragic passing. To be sure, he influence and sheer profundity of his contributions have touched, in some way or another, almost every jazz pianist working today.

Though inspired by be-bop ground breaker Bud Powell and the uncompromising single line creations of Lennie Tristano, Bill Evans found his own way and his own path and forever changed the way jazz piano is thought of. Evans brought an introspective, exploratory, harmonic depth to jazz and to the piano that simply was not there before. His use of modes, a.k.a. specific scales used to improvise–amply demonstrated on the *Kind of Blue* recording under the leadership of Miles Davis–opened new doors for the way jazz is played.

Despite his sphere of influence as a pianist and the way he could verbalize his feelings about music, away from the piano, Evans, who tragically passed away in 1980 at the age of 51, in was a shy, introverted loner who found solace through most of his life via the use of heroin and cocaine. While it is relatively easy to capture Bill Evans the artist on film—there is plenty of footage available—capturing the elusive man is another matter.

Film maker Bruce Spiegel, an award-winning producer/editor at CBS News/*48 Hours* for the past 25 years, has managed to do both in his incisive documentary on Evans, *Time Remembered: The Life and Music of Bill Evans.*

What makes this project so special is that it answers the question: Why is Bill Evans important? Spiegel addresses this with relatively straight forward, cinematic ease, interweaving some 40-plus interviews—some, sadly, with Evans cohorts and fans no longer with us—with film and sound clips of the man himself in performance, from his very early sessions as a sideman with players like clarinetist Tony Scott and multi-instrumentalist Don Elliott, to the latter-day work with his own trios and the two, ground-breaking recordings he made with Tony Bennett. Bennett's spoken contributions, as well as those from late drummer Paul Motian, writer Gene Lees and pianist Billy Taylor, to say nothing of the interviews with surviving family members, are particularly touching.

Spiegel's construction of the film is basically a chronological retelling of the most important professional and personal events in Bill Evans' life, and all of these events, as presented by the film maker, contributed substantially to Evans' depth of feeling and incomparable sense of invention as a player and composer. Some of the joyous events include Evans' evolution from sideman to leader, his significant contributions to *Kind of Blue*, exemplary work as a soloist, and his collaborations with Tony Bennett among them. The not-so-joyous events—the tragic death in a car accident of his young bassist Scott LaFaro, his drug addiction, and suicide of his wife and brother—are presented touchingly and factually.

What's missing from this generally first-rate piece of film making is at least one, complete performance from Bill Evans. Music documentaries, it seems, too often follow the dictum of interrupting an often captivating piece of music after a mere few second to cut to yet another talking head, no matter how interesting that talking head may be. Fortunately, taken as a whole, *Time Remembered: The Life and Music of Bill Evans* addresses and answers the most important question of them all: Why Bill Evans was and is important. – *Backstage, 2016.*

BUDDY DEFRANCO (1923-2015)

Buddy DeFranco, the Camden-born, South Philly-raised jazz clarinetist, was the first, and likely the best, artist to play modern jazz on an instrument that was not built for it.

His first instrument was, of all things, the mandolin, which he began playing at the age of five. Four years later, lucky for the world of jazz, he switched to clarinet. He attended Mastbaum School (then a music magnet school) in Philadelphia, where he was classically trained, and began in the jazz business when he won a national Tommy Dorsey talent contest. His entry into the world of name bands occurred when he was 16 years old with the big band of actor/singer/trumpeter Johnnie "Scat" Davis.

His reputation quickly grew. In 1943, he spent a few months with Krupa. The following year was his real breakthrough, when he joined the orchestra of the volatile trombonist Tommy Dorsey, whose ensemble was nicknamed "The General Motors of the Band Business." Swing clarinet was king in those days, given the fame of players like Benny Goodman and Artie Shaw, and DeFranco was right up there with them in terms of ability. things began to change when DeFranco heard bebop for the first time when he listened to recordings by Dizzy Gillespie, Charlie Parker, and others.

Dorsey could hear DeFranco practicing bop licks in the band room and didn't like it one bit. He demanded that the clarinetist play the exact same, note-for-note solos nightly, particularly on hit recordings like "Opus One." DeFranco just couldn't bear to repeat himself night after night. It was clearly time for him to move on, and he did so in 1948.

Early Buddy DeFranco

He signed with Capitol Records and recorded a marvelous series of bop sides, spent a few years in Count Basie's small group of the early 1950s, and later recorded a number of acclaimed tracks in small groups that included ultra-modernists like pianists Kenny Drew and Sonny Clark, accordionist Tommy Gumina, and drummer Art Blakey. He also recorded prolifically for Norman Granz's Verve Records, including a now-legendary date with piano giant Art Tatum.

Unfortunately, the clarinet – whether swing, bop, or otherwise – fell out of favor as the 1960s approached, and though DeFranco continued to win all the polls, he just wasn't getting the gigs. In 1966, he was offered a lucrative deal by the estate of Glenn Miller to take over leadership of the Miller "ghost" band (Miller died in 1944). Musically, it wasn't great. Financially, it was. DeFranco led the Miller band for eight years, and in 1974, realizing that the climate had again changed for his type of jazz – this time for the better – he decided to return to jazz full-time.

DeFranco didn't lose a beat and was better, more fluent, and more inventive than he ever had been, particularly when he teamed up with the swinging vibraphonist Terry Gibbs. As time went on, he was treated and regarded with reverence as a jazz giant and one of the few bonafide legends still on the scene. The annual Buddy DeFranco Jazz Festival at the University of Montana began in 1980. According to DeFranco's widow, Joyce, the fest will continue.

Of his playing, top jazz clarinet player Ken Peplowski said: "Buddy DeFranco almost single-handedly was the clarinetist who moved the harmonic and rhythmic language forward from where Benny Goodman left off."

As a person, DeFranco was one of the few in the world of jazz or elsewhere that you never, ever heard a bad word about. "Beautiful guy," was what you always heard. You can tell when you hear him play. It was always beautiful. – *Broad Street Review, 2015.*

NAT HENTOFF (1925-2017)

Nat Hentoff – journalist, author, civil rights advocate, "social commentator," and one of the most influential jazz writers in history – died on January 7, 2017 at the age of 91.

A controversial figure who wrote for the *Village Voice* for 50 years and authored 35 books, including works for young people, he was, by his own admission, "a troublemaker." *The New York Times* criticized his writing, saying it was not deeply researched and was mostly based on personal observation.

But despite his tremendous body of work as an author and in publications such as the *New Yorker* and *Washington Post*, his main contribution (and this point will likely be argued vigorously) was as a jazz writer who influenced subsequent generations of jazz writers, including yours truly.

Hentoff's interest in jazz began while attending public school in Boston. After working at a Boston radio station, in 1953 he moved to New York and wrote about jazz as a staffer for *DownBeat* magazine until 1957 (though he remained a contributor for many years). He founded the influential but short lived *Jazz Review*, which lasted from

1959 to 1960, before turning his attention to writing books, including his groundbreaking 1961 *The Jazz Life*, which detailed, for the first time in print, the social and psychological aspects of jazz.

Four years later, he wrote *Jazz Country*, a novel for youngsters that detailed the challenge of a young white musician's attempt to break into the jazz scene. I hadn't yet reached my teens when I read *Jazz Country*, but it is one of the reasons I got into jazz. In 1966, he wrote *Hear Me Talkin' To Ya*, an essential collection of interviews that, for the first time, featured five decades of jazz musicians speaking for themselves.

One might think Hentoff's jazz taste would be as progressive as his politics, but that wasn't the case. He embraced everyone from Gene Krupa to Charlie Mingus, but was a latecomer to modern jazz. According to Eric Tarloff, in writing about David Lewis's 2013 documentary, *The Pleasures of Being Out of Step: Notes on the Life of Nat Hentoff*, he initially had a tough time embracing be-bop.

"In Lewis's film," Tarloff says, "Hentoff relates a story that seems as extraordinary as it is characteristic of the man: unable to appreciate Charlie Parker's genius – the ideas were too dense and came to quickly for him to grasp, he says – he followed a friend's advice and listened to Parker's records at half speed, closely and repeatedly. Slowed down, the music gradually became comprehensible, its intricacies less opaque, its beauties less veiled, and he began to understand the scope of the talent on display."

Hentoff encouraged the involvement of young people in every facet of jazz, from performing to entrepreneurship. Suzanne Cloud, executive director and co-founder of Philadelphia's nonprofit The Jazz Bridge Project, which provides emergency funds and assistance for Philadelphia-area jazz and blues musicians, had an unforgettable interaction with Hentoff.

"He wrote the first piece on Jazz Bridge we ever had," Cloud recalls. "It was the first year our calendar came out, and I sent him one as he was writing the end page essay for *Jazz Times* magazine at the time. He loved it and wanted to find out more about Jazz Bridge and the calendar. He called me and, at first, I couldn't understand him on the phone. I asked, 'Who is this again?' And he yelled, 'It's Nat Hentoff! Hentoff! I'm on a deadline, dammit.' I told him not to yell at me, that even though I admired him immensely, he couldn't scream at me like that. He calmed down. Later, he called me back to apologize for being so abrupt. He was a wonderful writer on so many subjects and cheerleader for jazz."

That he was. – *Broad Street Review, 2017.*

GORDON "WHITEY" MITCHELL (1932-2009)

Gordon "Whitey" Mitchell, noted comedy writer and jazz bassist (yes, he was Red Mitchell's brother, as it said on Whitey's business card), has died at the age of 76. Mitchell first came to my attention by way of his work with The Gene Krupa Jazz Quartet. That particular edition of Gene's group, which lasted through much of 1955, included Gene, Whitey, Bobby Scott and Eddie Shu. It was one of Krupa's finest small units and fortunately, their concert sets at Jazz at the Philharmonic are well-preserved on CD.

Whitey performed with a bunch of other greats through the years, including Andre Previn, Mat Matthews, Gene Quill, Herbie Mann, Tony Scott, fellow bassist Oscar Pettiford, and J.J. Johnson. He recorded one session as a leader in 1956, and two years later, recorded with his brother and trumpeter Blue Mitchell on something aptly called *The Mitchells*. He left music in 1965 to work full time as a comedy writer.

As the story goes, several letters he wrote to DownBeat magazine came to the attention of no less than ground-breaking comic Lenny Bruce, who encouraged him to go into comedy writing. Starting in the mid-1960s, Whitey began writing for some of the legendary programs in television history, such as *Get Smart*, *The Jeffersons*, *All in the Family*, *Mork and Mindy*, *Good Times*, and *The Mary Tyler Moore Show*. If anyone ever wondered why several of those shows seemed to be so hip, *Get Smart* in particular, that was due in part to the efforts of Whitey.

Rare Whitey Mitchell LP, now fetching $200 on ebay

He moved to Palm Desert in the mid-1990s and began playing bass again. He was even better and more swinging than he was in 1955.

Some seasons back, I got a call from Whitey, who heard that I had some rare audio of his playing with the Krupa Quartet. We began talking on the telephone frequently, and I found him to be one of the most intelligent and literate folks I ever met. At the same time, I was thinking about going out to Palm Springs to do some archival video interviews with a bunch of industry people who relocated out there, including Buddy Rich's widow, Marie; and singer/entertainment executive Frankie Randall. Whitey spoke of how nice the jazz scene was in Palm Springs and Palm Desert, and that he had a great gig at a club there, which, if memory serves, was owned by a one-time *Playboy* Bunny. He said, "When you come out, get in touch and you'll sit in."

"Sit-in," to me, were and are the magic words. My now-ex and singing great Joy Adams and I decided to get out there as soon as possible. Whitey and his wife, Marilyn, were charming. We spent a good deal of time in their lovely home, and also a good deal of time in the jazz club where he was playing with a very swinging group.

One night at the club, it seemed that the crème de la crème of Palm Desert celebrity were seated at the table along with The Mitchells and us, including the legendary agent, Norby Walters and the equally famed singers and Palm Desert residents, Keely Smith and Jack Jones.

I remember specifically that Jones didn't crack a smile all night. Until, that is, Joy Adams sang. He told me later on in the evening, knowing that I wrote and co-produced the videos on Buddy Rich, that he never really got over Buddy's death and was never the same afterward.

To be asked to guest at the drums with Whitey Mitchell, a giant of a player , was an honor, especially because he had played with Krupa and always said how much he loved Gene's playing. He later told me how much he liked my playing and that there would always be work for Joy and me if we ever decided to move out to the desert.

After that, we lost touch. A month or two ago, someone told me he had written his autobiography, and I thought that would be an appropriate time to look him up again. I didn't, and I'm sorry about it.

I'll miss him. And so will jazz. – *Backstage, 2008.*

Note: Gordon "Whitey" Mitchell's autobiography, "Hackensack to Hollywood," was published by BearManor Media in 2007.

GEORGE BENSON MEETS NAT "KING" COLE

The parallels between the careers of the late pianist/singer Nat "King" Cole and guitarist/singer George Benson are astounding. Both initially made their mark in show business as jazz instrumentalists of the highest order. Cole was one of the most influential jazz pianists in history and Benson took the guitar legacy of Wes Montgomery to another level. Both later found incredible success in the pop field as singers, and Benson has said that his favorite singer was and is Cole.

Obviously, a George Benson salute to Cole show was entirely appropriate and in order.

George Benson: *An Unforgettable Tribute to Nat King Cole*, which played at the Philharmonic Center for the Arts in Naples, FL, was appropriate and in order. Unforgettable ? Most of the time.

Until his untimely death at the age of 45 in 1965, the singing voice of Nat Cole was among the most recognizable in show business and one of the most imitated. If you were an impressionist, you impersonated Cole. Sammy Davis Jr. could sound exactly like him. So could pianist Oscar Peterson, and if he's in the mood, Cole's still-active brother, Freddie, does Nat better than anyone. George Benson? The similarity between their voices is very, very close, though it's more of a strong influence than direct imitation. And Benson has been listening to Cole for a long time. Proof of that came via a snippet of a home recording played at the Phil, featuring the seven-year-old "Georgie" singing "Mona Lisa."

Benson bounded out on the Phil stage, not to the strains of a Cole song, but playing guitar on his own hit, 1976's "Breezin'," the first jazz record in history to go platinum and first in his amazing string of hits. Then the Cole tribute began in earnest with the grown-up Benson's version of "Mona Lisa," backed impeccably by a 28-piece string section, including some members from the Naples Philharmonic Orchestra, followed by another Cole biggie, "Nature Boy."

Cole's million-sellers were not all ballads, and the rhythmic, "Walkin' My Baby Back Home" was a good example.

Two of Cole's top-selling recordings were posthumous ones. "Unforgettable" and "When I Fall in Love" featured the voice of Cole's daughter, Natalie, electronically dubbed in, singing a duet with her late father. In a Los Angeles performance of this show Last month, Benson had a special guest star in the form of the wonderful singer, Patti Austin, a recent Grammy winner for her George Gershwin tribute CD. Her duets with Benson on those two songs were electric. At The Philharmonic, the partner was Janie Kluger, a member of the six-voice choir who joined the string section on some of the tunes. These duets could and should have come off better, as Kluger's voice seemed suited more to the Broadway stage than to the intimacy these songs require. Further, Benson seemed to be reading the words to many of the songs from an ill-placed music stand. Though each one was sung effectively in the Nat Cole style, the sincerity quotient suffered a bit. Maybe Benson needed more time to become comfortable with the material.

The choir was featured on "That Sunday, That Summer;" and Cole's biggest hit, "Ramblin' Rose." While these well-known songs received a tremendous response, the amplification of the six voices miked individually was way out of balance with the strings and the rhythm section. A few more moments at the sound check might have helped.

Pianist/conductor Randy Waldman, who led Barbra Streisand's orchestra for 20 years, proved to be an able conductor and a superior jazz pianist, with his keyboard featured on "Route 66" and "Straighten Up and Fly Right."

Benson, who proved to be a genial, quite funny and a very real master of ceremonies, continuously, promised the Phil audience that there would be a portion of the program devoted to a "George Benson party." This became a reality after he sang Cole's largest overseas hit, "Smile." Benson went into his very funky version of Cole's "Nature Boy," then the string section and choir left the stage. Mentioning his part-Welsh, part-Irish ancestry, he played a lovely guitar solo of "Danny Boy," proving that he still has few equals as a lyrical, jazz guitarist. Then, all the stops were pulled out. It was, as promised, party time.

Backed by two synthesizers, bass, drums and rhythm guitar, he switched into high gear on his own, fondly remembered, mega-recordings, including "Masquerade," "Turn Your Love Around," "Give Me the Light," and the beautiful "In Your Eyes" and "Nothing's Going to Change My Love for You." By the time he got to "Give Me the Light," the Phil audience was on its feet, clapping and stomping to the music, in the most enthusiastic display I've seen this season. This, evidently, is what the Philharmonic audience came to see and hear. The "real" George Benson voice, a combination of a funky Stevie Wonder, the mellowness of Johnny Mathis and even some overtones of Tom Jones (remember Benson's Welsh ancestry?) remains among the most individual in the music business.

In this 90-minute, 20-song show, George Benson was the total, energetic professional who never gave less than 100 percent of himself. But as a total, sum-of-all-its-parts program, I'd rate it a 97. And that's pretty good. – N*aples (FL) Daily News, 2009.*

Note: Benson revived his Nat Cole tribute show several times through the years in venues that could afford it. In 2013, he recorded the tribute, "Inspiration," for the Concord Jazz record label. It reached #89 on the Billboard charts.

IV
Give The Drummers Some

MEL TORMÉ ON GENE KRUPA

In the early 1980s, given the dearth of books about jazz on the market and the fact that there was very little out there about drumming pioneer Gene Krupa, I decided to write a book about Gene. All told, it took seven years to see the release of "World of Gene Krupa: That Legendary Drummin Man," published by Pathfinder Publishing of California. Despite my extensive work in newspapers and magazines, I was unknown as an author, and realized early on that if I could enlist the aid of a "celebrity name" in conjunction with the book, perhaps selling it to a publisher would be easier. Just before I began work on the book, I contacted Mel Tormé. Not only did Tormé worship Krupa, but Mel Tormé was quite appreciative of some articles I wrote about him, and we kept in touch. I asked him if he would have any interest in writing the introduction to a book I wanted to write about Krupa, though at that point, there was no publisher, no book, and only a plan to write one. Three weeks to the day after I contacted him, I received 10 typed pages in the mail from Mel Tormé. It was the introduction to my prospective book. Melvin Howard Tormé. What a guy!

Gene Krupa, mid-1950s

And here's Mel:

In 1940 I was 15 years old and growing up on the South Side of Chicago. Three blocks away from where I lived was a street called Kingston. One block up from Kingston there existed a corner grocery store, replete with green awning. I used to walk over to that store a few times a week, just to stare at the awning. On it, in faded white lettering were two names: LYKKE and KRUPA. Gene's family owned that store and the sheer magic of those five letters–K-R-U-P-A–acted upon me like a magnet.

Like every other aspiring young drummer in the country, the very mention of the words "Gene Krupa" conjured up images of excitement, glamour, jazz and that conglomerate of white pearl Slingerlands and burnished Zildjian cymbals that set this neophyte percussionist's heart soaring.

I had met Gene as a child, when I was appearing in kid vaudeville units around Chicago. He never spoke down to me, never treated me with anything other than kindness and encouragement. I started playing drums in Shakespeare Grammar School Drum and Bugle Corps when I was eight. By the time 1937 rolled around and Krupa had made history with Benny Goodman, I was as obsessed with being a drummer than any youngster in America.

Mel Tormé at the traps with Benny Goodman a Teddy Wilson, circa early 1950s

There is an old gag in our business. "Hey, man! Didja hear? Cootie left The Duke?" (Inevitably to evolve into "Chubby left Woody, etc.") When Gene left Benny to form his own band in 1938, it was no joke. Speculation was hot in our school. Would Gene make it as a bandleader? Who would he get to play in his band? And what about Benny? What? Davey Tough? Replacing Krupa? Oh yeah, he keeps great time, but...replacing KRUPA?

Krupa cost me a bike, the only one I ever had. My Aunt Ruth bought me a Roamer bicycle for me 13th birthday. My family, like every other Depression era family, felt the terrible squeeze of the fractured economy, and the bike like that was a genuine luxury. My best pal, Vic Grenock and I, took the Roamer on a shakedown cruise the Saturday following my birthday. Destination: The Tivoli Theater on Cottage Grove Avenue to see a new Bob Hope movie, *Some Like it Hot*. Debuting in that film was the brand new Gene Krupa Orchestra. I chained my bike to a lamp post right in front of the Tivoli. Vic and I sat through two shows, tapping our feet and pounding the seats in front of us to "Wire Brush Stomp" and "Some Like it Hot" and "This Lady's in Love with You" and "Jungle Madness." When we walked out of the darkened theater into the fading light, the Roamer was gone. Never another bike, but I saw that movie again and again. It turns up on TV occasionally, retitled Rhythm Romance for obvious reasons.

When I moved out to California with my folks, toward the end of World War II, the Hollywood Palladium was in full swing. Gene's band played regularly there, and every night I saw them there, and that was every night, Gene let me sit in with the band on drums. A red letter day (actually night) in my life was when he asked me to join the band as alternate drummer. By then I had a vocal group called the Mel Tones, and was unable to accept his offer. Wish I could have.

During the war, he had forsaken his now-famous heraldic bass drum monogram with the familiar "GK" painted in large, black, relief, and opted for a patriotically-devised rendering in red, white and blue, with bombers in the center of the head, encircled with the motto: "Let's Go America–Keep 'Em Flying." His drums took one hell of a beating, not only from his virile drumnastics, but from the constant travelling, setting up, breaking down of the set, the throwing of tom-toms and snare drum and bass drum in and out of fiber cases. Yet he seemed to retain the same set of drums for years at a time. When I asked him why he didn't order a new set from Slingerland, he smiled and said: "Are you kidding? These drums are just broken in." "These drums" were six years old. When I became a Slingerland user and endorser, "Bud" Slingerland and eventually Don Osborne, Sr. told me they had to practically beg Gene to accept new drum sets. He never took unfair advantage of the fact that he virtually "made" the Slingerland Drum Company, and that his name, over and above anyone else's, was SYNONOMOUS with the word "drums."

Gene Krupa was as much a gentleman as he was a musician. The men who worked for him happily attest to that. Unquestionably, he was eclectic. He gleaned from the likes of Zutty Singleton, Chick Webb and perhaps even Baby Dodds. Thing is, he developed a style of playing that was comprehensible and copyable. That's what most of the drummers of the day, particularly the white drummers, did. Buddy Schutz aped Gene. So did early Louis Bellson. Even young Buddy Rich incorporated several of Gene's "licks" in his outings with the Artie Shaw band in 1939. Like Ray McKinley, Jo Jones and Ray Bauduc, he was a highly musical drummer, not perhaps so much during his tenure with Benny, but afterward, with his own band.

In 1970, during a TV show in which we both participated, he told me how much he loved the music of Frederick Delius, an English composer who wrote, during the late 19th and 20th Century, some of the most beautiful orchestral music imaginable. Since Delius is, coincidentally, my favorite composer, Gene and I talked animatedly about him for over an hour. Gene was super knowledgeable on subject. He was really an appreciator and authority on music of all sorts, not merely a dabbler.

One night, in 1982, Benny Goodman came in to see me when I was appearing at a New York nightclub called Marty's. Between shows, I did something I always wanted to do; I sat and talked with BG for over an hour about the old days. I was surprised to learn that he did not particularly care for the convoluted, avant-garde arrangements during the "forties" period of his band; that he did like Mel Powell's playing, composing, and arranging was no great revelation. Fletcher Henderson was his all-time favorite arranger for the Goodman band and that the thirties band was closest to his heart.

Drummers?

How about Davey Tough, Benny? Harry Yeager? Buddy Shutz? Sid Catlett? Buddy Rich? Louis Bellson? They all played for you at one time or another. Who was the best?

Benny smiled patiently. "Gene. Gene was the best. There was no one like Gene."

Amen. – *Introduction to "World of Gene Krupa: That Legendary Drummin' Man" (Pathfinder Publishing of California), by Bruce Klauber, published 1990.*

BUDDY RICH: THE 1960-1961 FLUTE AND VIBES GROUP

The sometimes-bombastic Buddy Rich at the helm of a small group with a delicate front line of flute and vibes? Though it may be hard to believe for someone so closely associated with big bands, the truth is, a good deal of Rich's career was spent drumming in small combinations, as a leader and sideman. The flute and vibes group, featuring Sam Most and Mike Mainieri and varying rhythm sections, lasted from approximately April of 1960 through late 1961. The band was put together a few times after that, with the addition of saxophonist Georgie Auld, to fulfill a Las Vegas commitment.

Rich led a series of swinging small groups in 1958 and 1959, featuring players like alto saxophonists Phil Woods and Sonny Criss, trombonists Willie Dennis Ole Hansen, and pianist Kenny Drew. He also tried his hand at working nightspots as a singer, and had a disappointing vocal gig at The Living Room in New York City in October, 1959. All this swinging and singing, however, came to a screeching halt when Rich suffered a near-fatal heart attack, while appearing with the small band in the Dream Room Lounge in New Orleans.

Despite doctors orders that he not play for at least a year, Buddy Rich opened at Birdland with another small group after only four months after his illness.

Vibraphonist Mike Mainieri was there on opening night, hoping to sit in.

"A friend of mine was also a friend of Buddy's," Mainieri recalled. "He had been telling Buddy about me for years. Of course, Buddy said, 'What do I need with a vibes player? The last vibes player I had, Terry Gibbs, drove me crazy. I swore I'd never have another vibes player.'

"After Buddy played an entire set and then the second set, I was still waiting. He finally said to the audience, in his own endearing way, 'Well, ladies and gentlemen, we've got this kid in the audience who says he can play the vibes. Should we have him come up and play a tune with us?'

"Everyone went, 'Yeah, yeah!' So I went up there, set up my vibes in front of everyone, and he called off this amazingly fast tune. I don't remember what it was, but it was at a breakneck tempo, just to test me. He gave me the first solo, which was like 40 choruses long. At the end, everyone went nuts. I got a standing ovation and he hired me on the spot."

Rich was so impressed with Mainieri, that he also gave him free reign to arrange for the band and pick its members. Before the new flute/vibes band, with arrangements by Mainieri, came into existence, there was one recording commitment to fulfill. That Emarcy recording, called The Driver, was recorded on April 7 and 8, 1960, and featured the vibist along with Rich's regular small group.

Mike Mainieri was something of a child prodigy. In fact, he was 17 when he first joined Buddy Rich. In those days, his style was something of a modern version of Lionel Hampton, though less frenetic than Terry Gibbs, who had a mallet technique only equaled by Buddy Rich's speed with drumsticks.

In later years, he became one of the pioneers of jazz/rock with groups like Steps Ahead, and received a good deal of deserved notoriety for his work as a record producer for Carly Simon, among many, many others.

As a front line partner, Mainieri chose Sam Most, who worked in the big bands of Dorsey and Boyd Raeburn, and the small groups of Teddy Wilson and Teddy Charles. Most also doubled on clarinet, alto saxophone and piano, but his hard-driving flute playing is what attracted Mainieri and Rich. Buddy may have encouraged this instrumentation in a quest for a "more modern sound." To that end, it succeeded, but on Buddy Rich's terms.

Buddy Rich playing for his first big band, circa mid-1940s.

The band, while it existed, seemed to have done quite well in the popularity and booking sweepstakes. It found a virtual home at Birdland in New York City, appearing in July and October of 1960, and February, April, June and July of 1961. They also appeared frequently at the Cloister Inn in Chicago, did regular radio broadcasts and recorded two LPs, and in August of 1961, under President Kennedy's International Cultural Exchange Service, toured Afghanistan, Thailand, Cambodia, Laos, Indonesia, Hong Kong, South Vietnam and New Delhi, and Djakarta,

Of that trip, Buddy said, "Sure we were treated beautifully, but that was the worst experience of my life, man. I'd never seen such poverty, filth and starvation. It made you sick inside wherever you went. It tore your heart out." According to reports, Rich left the tour early without the rest of the band.

That turned out to be the last gig for the band. In January of 1962, Buddy Rich and Gene Krupa met in the Verve Record studios to record something called Burnin' Beat. Not long after, he again rejoined the sanctuary of the Harry James big band.

As for existing recordings of the flute/vibes group, after years of recording for Norman Granz' Verve label and its various imprints, Buddy had had it with the outspoken entrepreneur and left Granz shortly after the June, 1957, release of Buddy Rich in Miami, which featured tenor saxophonist Flip Phillips.

He believed he had found a more favorable situation with Mercury Records and Jack Tracy, and old friend who was director/producer of Mercury's new jazz director. Tracy gave Rich the freedom to do almost anything he wished, which included a meeting with Max Roach, a big band project, small group recordings and vocal albums. It's not surprising that when Tracy left Mercury for the relatively new, Chicago-based Argo label, Rich went him.

The LP called Playtime was recorded on October 3, 1960, about two weeks after the small group appeared at Chicago's Cloister Inn, located within the hotel Maryland.

In January, shortly after appearing on Playboy's Penthouse television program, the group recorded another album's worth of material for what was to be Argo #683. For reasons still unknown, those sides were never released. Strangely, the last recording done by this combination, with the addition of trumpeter Rolf Ericson, was done for Verve Records in August of 1961. Rich nemesis Norman Granz had sold–or was about to sell–Verve.

Though relatively short-lived, the Rich/Mainieri/Most groups personified everything that jazz is and that jazz can be. Thankfully, those bands and its members are finally getting the recognition due them. And Buddy Rich? He drove and fired up and electrified every type of ensemble, of every size and style for almost seven decades. We will never see or hear another like him. – *Notes to the Fresh Sound Records CD, "Playtime." – 2011.*

BUDDY RICH AT 100

The January 2017 issue of *DownBeat* magazine, that venerable journal of jazz that has been published continuously since 1934, paid tribute to four jazz legends who would have been 100 years old in 2017: pianist Thelonious Monk, trumpeter John Birks "Dizzy" Gillespie, vocalist Ella Fitzgerald, and "the world's greatest drummer," Buddy Rich (1917-1987).

Buddy Rich publicity shot, mid-1970s.

The inclusion of Rich is both interesting and appropriate. Though never an innovator like the other *DownBeat* honorees, something Rich himself admitted, he nonetheless had a remarkable career. As writer John McDonough in his essay on the fiery drummer and bandleader has detailed, Rich's seven-decade career began in the vaudeville era, and progressed to swing, bop, fusion, and rock. There is not a legend of jazz he did not play or record with, including fellow *Downbeat* honorees Ella, Diz and Monk. Buddy Rich's "innovations" were versatility and an ability to evolve, a rarity in jazz.

Sure, there were and are other great drummers, but several things set him apart. If Superman decided to play the drums, he still could not surpass what Rich could play on a drum set. His technique has never been equaled or surpassed, and it likely never will be.

As an accompanist – and he accompanied everyone from Louis Armstrong to Art Tatum – the man was an unparalleled inspiration. His feel went way beyond swing. With Buddy behind a soloist (members of his latter-day bands would be happy to corroborate this), a player could not help but play way over his or her head.

His controversial 1966 decision to form his own big band came during a time it was thought big bands were virtually dead. However, he helped inspire renewed interest in big bands, paving the way for the increased popularity of Basie, Ellington and Kenton, and new ensembles like the Thad Jones/Mel Lewis Jazz Orchestra, and the comeback of Maynard Ferguson.

Finally, as writer McDonough pointed out, "Thirty years after his death, Buddy Rich remains the most famous drummer in jazz history. People who know nothing about the music know that the words 'Buddy Rich' and 'drums' have become synonymous."

Credit for Rich's continued popularity should go to talk show host Johnny Carson, who helped establish Rich as a tart-tongued "personality" like Don Rickles, a persona that made jazz lovers out of folks who might not otherwise have been interested in the music. And Buddy's daughter, Cathy, has worked tirelessly to perpetuate her father's legacy with the continuation of the Buddy Rich band, with Gregg Potter at the drums, B.R. Memorial Scholarship Concerts, reissues, newly discovered audios and videos, and more.

Like many drummers of my generation, I'm not ashamed to say Rich was my idol, so my part in the production of *Buddy Rich: Jazz Legend*, produced with daughter Cathy and widow Marie, was quite the emotional experience. I took Cathy aside at one point and asked her father what he would have thought of a project like this. "He would have loved it," she said. I hope so. – *Broad Street Review, 2016.*

"THE VIEW FROM THE BACK OF THE BAND: THE LIFE AND MUSIC OF MEL LEWIS"

In the history of jazz drumming, there was a time when certain drummers were instantly identifiable. A listener could tell, after just a few measures, whether the drummer playing was Gene Krupa, Max Roach, Buddy Rich, Art Blakey and several others. One of that very special group was Mel Lewis, now the subject of a superb biography via University of North Texas Press, titled *The View From The Back Of The Band: The Life and Music of Mel Lewis.*

Mel Lewis and Thad Jones

Author Chris Smith, a drummer and jazz educator, has beautifully interwoven the man, born Melvin Sokoloff, and the music, by way of interviews with just about everyone living who knew Lewis, and a bunch of now-rare though previously published material, and extensive radio interviews with the man himself. For the drummers out there, Smith has included several musical transcriptions and an overview of Lewis' equipment through the years, which was essential to the unique and singular sounds he was able to get from his drums and cymbals.

Curiously, the man who recorded almost 700 records and drove the bands of Stan Kenton, Terry Gibbs, Gerry Mulligan and dozens of small groups, had next-to-no technique in the traditional sense of the word. No, his drum roll might not have been the greatest, but he knew what his job was: To accompany, to inspire, and above all, to be musical.

Though outspoken and brutally honest, he remained dedicated to the purity of jazz, whatever the setting. Lewis had a remarkable professional career on record, in the studios, with big bands and small groups. But at the age of 37, he formed an alliance with writer/arranger/trumpeter Thad Jones that forever changed the course of how jazz is played by large ensembles. The "Thad Jones/Mel Lewis Orchestra" was a true jazz orchestra that effectively combined extended soloing–by some of the best players in New York–with the written arrangements. Originally, "Thad and Mel" started playing at New York City's Village Vanguard every Monday night–and many aspiring Philadelphia jazz musicians were there every Monday–but evolved into a road band that toured the world.

Mel Lewis and Gene Krupa rehearsing for 1979 Canadian television special

Then in January of 1977, the unthinkable happened. Telling almost no one, Jones abruptly left the band to settle in Denmark. The author reveals that Jones' reasons for leaving–an event that shocked the jazz world–were that he was disillusioned with the state of music in the United States, and that the married Jones had met another woman in Denmark. Indeed, he later married that woman not too long after he set up residence there.

No matter. Mel Lewis bravely carried on as the band's leader, often staffing the band with younger players and writers who were just beginning to make their marks in the world of jazz. He heroically kept the band going until losing, at age 60 in 1990, his battle with cancer. The band, now called the Vanguard Jazz Orchestra, continues playing every Monday night as it has for an astounding 48 years, at the Village Vanguard. Mel Lewis would be pleased.

Mel Lewis influenced a load of drummers, including yours truly, not only in terms of style, but in terms of honesty and integrity when it comes to jazz. Philadelphia bandleader/drummer Phil Giordano, a dear friend and student of Mel Lewis, could only sum up Lewis' contributions by saying, "Mel was all music." – *Modern Drummer magazine, 2014.*

NICK FATOOL (1915-2000)

Swing era drummers like Gene Krupa, Buddy Rich, "Papa" Jo Jones, Dave Tough, "Big" Sid Catlett, Cozy Cole, Chick Webb and Ray McKinley might have received most of the publicity and critical acclaim, but few drummers of any era played so well, so long and with so many than Nick Fatool.

Fatool, in a career that spanned six decades, was a schooled and versatile player, equally adept at swinging a big band, playing traditional jazz, working in the studio, on film sound tracks and in live shows. His sound was crisp, clear and clean. When listening to those "big band re-creation" projects he recorded in the 1950s with Glen Gray, it is evident that he paid a lot of attention to tuning the drums. The snare, toms and bass were tuned for maximum resonance, not easy with calf heads back then. He was able to get everything possible, sound-wise, out of every drum. When necessary, like on those big band tribute dates, he could sound like anyone.

Stylistically, he wasn't a pacesetter on the scale of "Papa" Jo or "Big Sid," nor was he a technical marvel ala Krupa and Rich. Though he listened to them all, and it was very clear he was inspired by the traditional drumming of Ray Bauduc, Fatool came in and did his job with a minimum of fuss. And what jobs they were.

Born in Milbury, Massachusetts, on January 2, 1915, Fatool's early gigs were local ones, played around Providence, Rhode Island, area. At the age of 22, he realized that re-locating to New York City was a necessity for anyone serious about the music business. Starting in 1937, he performed with the bands of Joe Hyams, George Hall and Don Beston. As good as those groups may have been, those bandleaders were not gigantic industry names.

Nick Fatool, early 1950s

Benny Goodman, a.k.a. "The King of Swing," always had a hard time with drummers, never really knowing what he wanted from them. Remember, this was the guy who fired "Big" Sid Catlett, let Krupa and Dave Tough go, gave Mel Lewis a hard time and wouldn't give the time of day to Buddy Rich. When Krupa left to form his own band in 1938, Goodman went through a succession of fine drummers including Tough and Buddy Shutz. After playing for a short time with trumpeter Bobby Hackett in 1939, Fatool was asked to join the hottest band in the country, Benny Goodman and his Orchestra. He stayed for two years.

During this period, Fatool participated in a series of legendary and ground-breaking recordings with what was to be the first "Benny Goodman Sextet," the group that introduced guitar genius Charlie Christian to the world.

As usual, BG treated a number of his men poorly, including his drummer. Star Goodman trumpeter Chris Griffin told author Ross Firestone in the book *Swing Swing Swing: The Life & Times of Benny Goodman*, "Outside of Dave Tough, Nick Fatool was the best drummer we ever had as far as playing with and for the band." But according to saxophonist Jerry Jerome, "For some reason, Benny just wasn't satisfied and he started giving Nick 'The Ray' (Goodman's cold, intense and unrelenting manner of staring at a player in order to humiliate and intimidate him) when we were recording in California. During the rehearsal he said to him, 'Lay out while we do this,' which is a normal thing to do, and after we finished rehearsing without the drums, he had Nick come back in and play. But then he had him lay out again, and this time he turns around and says to the band, 'You know, I think it sounds better this way.' Now whether Benny meant this cruelly or whether this particular thing we were doing did sound better without the drums, I don't know, but Nick wanted to cut off his head with a cymbal. He was absolutely furious at being humiliated like that, and he subsequently left." Such were the strange ways of "Mr. Warmth," and the master of diplomacy, Benny Goodman.

Goodman's rival in those days was the enigmatic clarinetist/bandleader Artie Shaw. Fatool spent most of 1941 and 1942 with Shaw, then billed as "The King of the Clarinet." The drum chair with Shaw's crew wasn't an easy one. Bear in mind that that none other than Buddy Rich was Shaw's drummer in latter 1938 and much of 1939. Like Goodman, Shaw wasn't easy, either.

By the time he was 25 years of age, Nick Fatool could say that he stepped into positions once occupied by Gene Krupa and Buddy Rich. That's how big his talents were.

He marked some time in the early 1940s, joining the popular though non-swinging band of Jan Savitt in 1942, and the innovative Claude Thornhill organization the same year. He spent 1942 and 1943 with the advanced ensemble of guitarist Alvino Rey.

Fatool was, in retrospect, quite the visionary. He realized, at that early time, that the industry's future was going to be Los Angeles-based and in the recording studio. He got his ticket to the coast by touring with Harry James' band in 1943, and began doing studio work. He was one of the busiest session players through the 1950s, recording with artists that included Louis Armstrong, pianists Erroll Garner and Jess Stacy, trumpeter Billy Butterfield, big band leaders Glenn Gray, Tommy Dorsey and Billy May, singers Billie Holiday, Jo Stafford, Peggy Lee, Nat "King" Cole, Dean Martin, Gordon MacRae, Frank Sinatra, The Andrews Sisters, Margaret Whiting and Betty Hutton. Yes, he's even on record backing Robert Mitchum and Andy Griffith!

He played on the film soundtracks of *Pete Kelly's Blues* (1955) and *The Five Pennies* (1959), the latter a highly fictionalized version of the life of trumpeter Red Nichols. Fatool can actually be seen in action with Artie Shaw via his on-screen in *Second Chorus* (1940).

By 1958, he seemingly began to tire of the studio grind, and session-wise, the mainstream, playing and singing pop artists were gradually being replaced by rock and roll artists.

In the midst of a 1956 to 1958 stint playing on Bing Crosby's radio program, Fatool returned to live performing with Bing's brother, singer/bandleader Bob Crosby. That was the beginning of a more than 30-year identification with traditional/dixie-oriented jazz and jazz drumming. Though he came from a big band and studio background, his "traditional" chops were as good as Bauduc, Zutty Singleton and the rest. One can hear a good deal of Baby Dodds in his playing as well.

Bob Crosby did have a big band—and small group within, named the Bobcats—but they played a type of "orchestrated Dixieland" that was innovative and wildly successful. Their biggest hit was "Big Noise From Winnetka," first played by Crosby bassist Bob Haggart and drummer Ray Bauduc.

As a singer, Bob was no Bing, but he was a good-natured and effective front man who let his personnel do what they did best. Fatool was in and out of the Crosby fold for years: from 1957 to 1959 in clubs and concerts in the states, then on a Far East tour in 1964, followed by a tenure in Vegas with Crosby and comic Phil Harris from 1969 to 1973, and a final overseas tour in 1981. Audiences may have thought that Nick Fatool was Ray Bauduc, in that he must have had to reprise "Big Noise From Winnetka" hundreds of times.

As if he wasn't busy enough, Fatool became a golf pro in 1972.

Clarinetist Pete Fountain was one of the biggest names in traditional jazz, having first come to fame as a part of Lawrence Welk's television family in 1958. Fountain's time with Welk and his many appearances on *The Tonight Show Starring Johnny Carson*, helped put Fountain on the map as an international name. Musically, Fatool and Fountain were perfect for each other. The two joined forces in Fountain's native New Orleans from 1962 to 1965, and again from 1967 to 1969.

The 1970s saw the drummer playing with other traditionalists, including trumpeter Dick Cary and clarinetists Matty Matlock and Peanuts Hucko. During this period, he also played briefly with the ever-popular Dukes of Dixieland.

In the 1980s, he was very active on the Dixieland revival/festival circuit. Though it doesn't get a lot of national exposure, with the exception being bandleader/cornetist Jim Cullum's *Riverwalk Jazz* radio broadcast on National Public radio, Dixieland is as popular as ever today. The number of nationwide festivals and the music's numbers of fans, is astounding.

Unbelievably, it was not until 1987 that he recorded his first project as a leader, a trad date that included tenor saxophonist Eddie Miller and clarinetist Johnny Mince and released on the Jazzology label.

With the death of Nick Fatool on September 26, 2000, the world of jazz percussion lost its last, "authentic," dixieland drummer. Sure, dixie is as popular today and there are some great, young dixieland drummers around. But none of them play like Nick Fatool. – *Modern Drummer magazine, 2013.*

LOUIE BELLSON (1924-2009)

Louie Bellson, master drummer, composer, arranger, educator and the last of the certifiable swing era percussion stars, passed away on February 14 at the age of 84.

As a player and as a human being, he was a one-of-a-kind. Whether at a clinic, a master class, recording session, or after a performance, he took the time to answer every question, sign every autograph, and fulfill every request. He spoke ill of no one. No one.

His playing was just like he was: beyond category, eras or labels. Stylistically, his was an "all-purpose" way of playing that fit with everything. Though grounded in swing, and indeed, his first major job was with Benny Goodman, this was an artist who played with everyone from Louis Armstrong and Harry James to Charlie Parker and Dizzy Gillespie. Technically, most percussion experts agree that he was, possibly along with Joe Morello, the only one who could come close to equaling Buddy Rich's speed and dexterity. His ground-breaking use of two bass drums took Buddy's technique a step beyond.

Whatever he played, and no matter what the setting, he never let his technique get in the way of taste. He played for the situation, and in his long and varied career, "the situation" included a lot of session work, backing the likes of Sammy Davis, Jr. and Tony Bennett, subbing in *The Tonight Show* orchestra, or acting as musical director for his first wife, entertainer Pearl Bailey.

Born Luigi Paulino Alfredo Francesco Antonio Balassoni on July 6, 1924, in Rock Falls, Illinois, Bellson's interest in drums began at the age of three. As a teen, he came up with the idea of using a second bass drum as a part of the drum kit and in fact, his design for it won him an "A" in high school art class (the problem was getting a drum company to build a kit to his specs, until the Gretsch Drum Company stepped forward several years later). In 1941, he won the national Gene Krupa Drum Contest sponsored by Slingerland drums, beating out—literally and figuratively-- more than 40,000 other drummers.

Louie Bellson, European tour, 1979

His first major job was with the big band of Ted FioRito, until Benny Goodman grabbed him in 1942. During the 1940s, he spent most of his time in the bands of Goodman and Tommy Dorsey, with several time outs to lead his own small groups.

In the early 1950s, Louie Bellson made history.

In 1951, Duke Ellington was running into problems. Three of his biggest stars—drummer Sonny Greer, alto saxophonist Johnny Hodges and trombonist Lawrence Brown--left Duke to work in a small group led by Hodges. The savvy Ellington raided the Harry James band that year—the caper was known as "the great James robbery"—and enticed altoist Willie Smith, valve trombonist Juan Tizol and drummer Bellson to join the Ellington band. The drummer, the first, permanent Ellington band member who was white, is generally credited as reviving Duke's band and inspiring it to swing like it never did before. And, Duke encouraged Bellson's composing and arranging talents, performing and recording what became two, Duke Ellington hits, "Skin Deep" and "The Hawk Talks."

A year later, he made national headlines when he married entertainer Pearl Bailey. In 1952, tolerance for interracial marriage was not at a particularly high level in this country, and those early years spent in the public spotlight, were not easy for them. Still, the union flourished and lasted until Bailey's death in 1990.

Over the years, he returned to the Ellington fold from time to time on an as-needed basis, often for Duke's special Sacred Concerts. Likewise, he frequently deputized in the bands of Count Basie, Harry James, Woody Herman and countless others.

In the 1970s and 1980s, he became more involved in leading – and composing and arranging for–his own orchestras, and in the jazz education movement. He's written over a dozen drum instruction books and participated in a number of videos. Since the 1970s, he's been the recipient of numerous awards, among the first being named a "Duke Ellington Fellow" by Yale University in 1977.

He continued playing, composing and recording until just a few months before his death, with his final CD being a collaboration with trumpeter Clark Terry.

Hudson Music and yours truly were involved in a number of performance-oriented and instructional projects with Louie Bellson through the years. He added wonderful commentary on the *Gene Krupa: Jazz Legend* video project, and he narrated the monumental, *Legends of Jazz Drumming* videos. Along with Roy Haynes, Elvin Jones and Max Roach, he was the subject of the 1998 *Zildjian Lifetime Achievement Awards* videos. Whatever the project, he was, without exception, knowledgeable, thoughtful, enthusiastic, tireless, encouraging, funny, and always swinging. In one marathon session of filming. Bellson commented on almost 100 drummers in jazz history, including a number of contemporary players. He knew what they all contributed, and spoke of how they all were and are important.

Like Gene Krupa, Bellson was a perpetual student, always listening and always learning. Personally? He personified the world "gentleman." Whenever we saw each other, he always told me how important my work was and how much of a contribution I continued making. He made people feel good about themselves and what they were doing.

Louie Bellson is survived by his wife, Francine, who helped guide her husband's career since their marriage in 1991. "Francine has been a blessing to me," Bellson said some years back. "I'm a man who got two blessings–with Pearl 38 years and I thought that was the end but–here comes Francine. She's been so great. When Pearl passed away, the first two years I was okay during the day, but at nighttime when I wasn't performing, I was lonesome. All of sudden Francine came, and I thought I was hallucinating. But she brought me back to reality again."

Rest in peace, Maestro. And keep swingin'. –*Backstage, 2009.*

RUFUS "SPEEDY" JONES (1936-1990)

"The first time we heard Rufus 'Speedy' Jones was when he was with Count Basie. Rufus had been given big solo spots, and his explosive rhythms and animation came off in very convincing, symbolic patterns. His horizontal movements—straightforward and circular—from cymbal to cymbal, along with his eyes and eyeglasses, all seemed to play a part in his mysticalizationalist's paradiddled self-portrait tapestry.

"Since Rufus Jones has been with us, his supporting role, particularly in African, jungle, and oriental pieces, has constantly led to demands from the audience for him to be featured solo. Just as constantly, his drum solos have been showstoppers that result, half the time, in standing ovations.

"Mostly a vegetarian, he is a good, clean-living guy, and a karate expert. As a man, he is easy to get along with and to respect. He is the 'Cat Anderson of all Rufuses.'"

– Duke Ellington

There was a time in percussion history when speed–though not necessarily everything–nonetheless played a big part in just what made a drummer a big name. Fans loved debating such things: Was it Krupa, Rich, Bellson, Roach, Morello, or even Barrett ("The World's Fastest Drummer") Deems who held the speed record?

A very good case would have to be made for one of the most unsung and under-appreciated, and certainly among the absolute fastest, drummers in the history of jazz.

Though Jones sparked some of the legendary ensembles in jazz history, including those of Maynard Ferguson, Lionel Hampton, Count Basie and Duke Ellington, he remains relatively unknown, and material available on him is scarce. "Why" is a mystery. This was a player who had it all.

The Charleston, S.C., native first started on trumpet in grammar school, then switched to drums at the age of 13. Five years later, at college age, he was deemed talented enough to be awarded a scholarship at Florida A&M University.

His "formal" university affiliation didn't last long, as Jones decided to join the University of Lionel Hampton. He first recorded with the ebullient vibraphone master in Germany, in 1954.

From there, circa 1958, he became a regular at New York city's rowdy, jazz showplace, The Metropole Café, backing swing era stalwarts like Sol Yaged and Henry "Red" Allen, and rubbing elbows with Metropole regulars like drummers Gene Krupa and Cozy Cole.

A year later, he made his breakthrough with what was then the hottest, most popular band in the land, that of trumpeter Maynard Ferguson's.

For those familiar only with trumpeter Ferguson's jazz/rock/pop/fusion groups of the 1970s onward, the trumpeter's late 1950s and early 1960s bands will be a revelation.

Ferguson could blow higher and louder than any trumpet player in history, and his band, only 13 strong, reflected the leader's preference for volume, speed and high drama. Make no mistake about it. This was a jazz band.

Jones' drumming held the whole thing together. His "organic" tuning of the traps made the drums an integral part of the band, much like another member of the trombone section. Given the limited instrumentation, Jones felt it necessary that the drums "fill in the gaps," sound-wise," left by the absence of fourth trumpet, third bone or fifth reed. It worked, and at the same time, he managed to swing that band into bad health.

The drum chair in MF's band was a challenging one. Legendary charts like "Stella by Starlight" and "The Mark of Jazz" were literally all over the place, with drum fills required every few bars. Rufus made it sound seamless.

He was a master of slow tempi as well, evidenced by his playing on Slide Hampton's famed "Frame for the Blues." Few could swing a band, of this or of any instrumentation, at this slower-than-slow tempo.

Rufus stayed in this hot drum chair until 1963, spelled at various times by Jake Hanna and Frankie Dunlop, when the fortunes of the Ferguson band began to change.

One time Basie drummer Butch Miles recalled seeing and hearing Jones at this time.

"I was all of 16 and marching with my high school band in the Macy's Thanksgiving Day Parade in New York," Miles remembered. "We had one night with a fairly late curfew so I–being the hip, young swinging, musician–organized a trip for six of us on the town finishing up at Birdland where Buddy Rich and his sextet were performing with Maynard Ferguson's big band. Wound up there for the last two or three tunes of Buddys' group and nearly didn't stay for Maynard. I really had gone only to hear Buddy and didn't know much about MF but to this very day I'm glad I stayed. Maynard's drummer was a young man by the name of Rufus Jones and what he played that night almost made me quit playing drums. SPEED, speed and more speed and all of it done with great ease. I never (and rarely since) saw a roll that high up off of the snare. His hands went over his head. Unbelievable. And SWINGING?

"From that night long ago I became a huge Rufus 'Speedy' Jones fan and I still am. I will never, ever forget what I saw and heard that Thanksgiving night in 1960. Mr. Jones has never received the recognition due an artist of his stature. He sure opened my ears, though."

Jones led his own small group from 1963 to 1964, recording his only opus as a leader in 1964 for the Cameo Parkway label, entitled "Five on Eight," which remains one of the most obscure items in the history of the jazz LP. Maynard, by the way, was recording for Cameo at this time, and may have helped Jones get this date as a leader.

Rufus "Speedy" Jones, Ellington days

He marked time for another year as a member of the Apollo Theater House band–again, not an easy gig–and joined Hampton again briefly before joining Duke Ellington's band, without doubt, the most famous jazz orchestra there ever was.

In late 1966, when Rufus Jones took over from Sam Woodyard, Jones probably switched to the two bass drum set up that Duke required of all his drummers since Louie Bellson's arrival in 1951.

Like Bellson and Woodyard before him, the drummer got his share of crowd-pleasing solo spots with the Duke. Jones' contributions to Hudson Music's Classic Drum Solos DVDs, give an accurate idea of just how speedy Rufus was.

Though he doesn't exploit the two bass drums ala Bellson, his single strokes, combined, as the Duke mentioned, with plenty of paradiddling, were simply incredible. His speed, dexterity and ability to move effortlessly between each part of the kit, is just amazing to watch and to hear. In terms of stamina, one gets the sense that he could go on doing this for hours, without breaking a sweat. That he never wrote an instructional book was a crime.

The only downside, if there is one, is that Jones' "organic" tuning sometimes blurred just what audiences heard. It wasn't that he lacked rudimental articulation, it was simply that, because of how the drums sounded, one note blurred into the next, often making it sound like one, long roll. Drummers, however, knew better, and audiences still ate it up.

Like the band of Ferguson, Duke's band had its own set of complexities. It was a band of difficult, individual personalities–and with no drum book, to boot–and it was to Rufus' credit that he stayed until 1973.

Probably his biggest and most memorable contribution to the Duke Ellington band was his participation in the recording of Duke's *Far East Suite.*

In the mid-1960s, Ellington began concentrating, more and more on large scale works and longer forms with titles like "Suite Thursday" and his sacred concerts. Some of them worked and some didn't. *Far East Suite* did, as most of the suite was actually a series of concertos for Duke's stellar soloists.

Rufus Jones helped make it successful as well. He brought a more pointed and cleaner sound than Sam Woodyard did, to say nothing of the sensitive, oriental effects required. Bearing in mind that there were no drum charts and that this was Jones' first recording with Ellington, just makes *Far East Suite* more remarkable.

Taken as a whole, the result is beautifully hypnotic. And though Duke hardly ever performed any of the suite's pieces in person, one title, "Isfahan" became a standard.

Far East Suite is available on a Bluebird, digipak CD, with a bunch of bonus tracks.

Rufus Jones played on a number of Ellington's best, latter day recordings, including *70th Birthday Concert* (Solid State), *New Orleans Suite* (Atlantic), and a small group effort that shows just how sensitive the drummer could be, *The Pianist* (Fantasy).

One of the more amazing things about Duke was his ability to hold on to many of his stellar soloists for so many years. Equally incredible is that, in over 40 years as a band leader, the turnover in the drum chair was minimal. Yes, there were subs, as there are in any big band–and Duke's subs included names like Steve Little, Ben Riley, Max Roach, Panama Francis, Butch Ballard, Ed Shaughnessy, Jimmy Johnson and Chris Columbus–but on a permanent basis, only Sonny Greer, Louie Bellson, Dave Black, Sam Woodyard and Rufus Jones were in for the long term. That is a tribute to them all.

Rufus Jones' post-Ellington life was heartbreaking. Reports are that Jones suffered from crippling arthritis and had to leave Ellington in the summer of 1973, as he found it harder and harder to play. He was replaced by drummer Rocky White, said to be the last drummer that Duke personally hired. Duke Ellington died on May 24, 1974.

In 1987, Jones' mentally challenged son, Lebrew, was wrongfully convicted of a murder that was said to have taken place on a construction site where Lebrew worked. He was convicted in 1989. The conviction was overturned in November of 2009, after Lebrew served 20 years in prison.

His father did not live to see his son's conviction overturned. Rufus Jones died on April 25, 1990. He spent his final years, according to various sources, including the great Las Vegas drummer Paul Testa, working as a porter and men's room attendant at Caesars Palace in Las Vegas.

Rufus Jones could and should have spent his last years teaching master classes, lecturing or writing instructional books. Why no one in the musical community stepped forward on his behalf remains a question.

What doesn't remain a question is that Rufus "Speedy" Jones, speed aside, was one of the most flexible, sensitive, understanding and swinging drummers who ever played. – *Modern Drummer magazine, 2014.*

ED SHAUGHNESSY: "LUCKY DRUMMER, FROM NYC JAZZ TO JOHNNY CARSON"

Ed Shaughnessy

Ed Shaughnessy at early 1960s "Tonight Show" rehearsal

Perhaps Gene Krupa, Buddy Rich and Ringo Starr were more famous, but no drummer in music history was more visible than Ed Shaughnessy (1929-2013). With rare exception, he appeared on network television five nights per week for an astounding 29 years, as the drummer in the big band led by Carl "Doc" Severinsen for *The Tonight Show Starring Johnny Carson.*

In his new autobiography, *Lucky Drummer: From NYC Jazz to Johnny Carson* (Rebeats Publishing) written with Robyn Flans, Shaughnessy tells of his decades with Doc, the jazz years that led up to that fabled gig, of the stars of jazz and jazz drumming with whom he's worked, and of a personal life that, in some cases, was challenging.

The book, like its author, is a charmer. *Lucky Drummer* is touching, funny, informative and educational, honest though not brutally so, and at times heartbreaking. *Lucky Drummer* also serves as a guidebook for anyone who plays, or has wanted to play, drums professionally.

Though he claims he wasn't really a percussion innovator or ground-breaker, truth be told, the pre-*Tonight Show* Shaughnessy backed some of the most progressive players in jazz. Those included vibist Teddy Charles, the larger-than-life bassist/composer Charles Mingus, tenor saxophonist-turned-Miles Davis-producer Teo Macero, odd time signature master Don Ellis, sitar player Ravi Shankar and tabla artist Alla Rakha, and the entire Marsalis Family.

On the more traditional end of the spectrum, the author played and recorded with Basie, Ellington, Benny Goodman, Tommy Dorsey, Wes Montgomery, George Benson, Jimmy Smith, Quincy Jones, Billie Holiday and dozens of others. What a resume! The names on these lists, by the way, do not include the hundreds of players and singers he accompanied during his tenure on *The Tonight Show*.

Those in the business, as well as the hundreds of students he's taught and mentored, can attest that, along with his friend Louie Bellson, Ed Shaughnessy was one of the nicest people out there, in any field.

Naturally, he shares plenty of stories about "the cats." He could have easily been negative about several of them, but as always, he's taken the high road. His yarns about Anita O'Day, Buddy Rich, Benny Goodman, Jimi Hendrix, Mingus and Miles are often hilarious. The author could have been a lot more harsh when writing about how he was treated by a nasty Ray Charles. As is his wont, Shaughnessy goes relatively easy on "the genius."

Especially gratifying is the space he gives to saxophonist/bandleader Charlie Ventura, Shaughnessy's first "big name" employer. This is the first book to deservedly address Ventura's talents and contributions.

When this book was published, Ed Shaughnessy was 83 years old and was still out there playing, and playing very well. And after all those years, as he said, "The door is open, any time you see me and would like to talk. I've always been that way, and I will always be that way. I really love to talk with–and help, if I can–any younger musicians who come my way. I never forget that everybody did it for me." – *Backstage, 2012*

"JAKE HANNA: THE RHYTHM AND WIT OF A SWINGING JAZZ DRUMMER"

Woody Herman led a band for six decades, and in those six decades, granted complete musical freedom to only two sidemen: Drummers Dave Tough and Jake Hanna. Because of their taste, time, ability to swing, support and play for the band, the Old Woodchopper let them play any way they wanted. In the process, Tough and Hanna became legends.

There's a new book out about one of those legends, Jake Hanna, and it stands as essential reading. For anyone who can read.

Maria S. Judge, Hanna's niece, has written her uncle's biography, *Jake Hanna: The Rhythm and Wit of a Swinging Jazz Drummer* (Meredith Music Publications) and like the subject, the work is as much a "production" as it is a bio. That's because Hanna, who sadly left us in 2010, was quite the multi-faceted "production" himself, fondly remembered as a story teller, humorist, sports fan, family man, teacher, mentor, talent scout, and a versatile percussionist who virtually stood for the concept of swing.

Obviously, a regular bio could not do in this extraordinary case, which is why Ms. Judge enlisted the contributions of, count 'em, 192 friends, fans, family members, fellow musicians, students and admirers. As a whole, they tell of the drummers' many sides, ranging from genial family man and uncompromising musician, to rabid sports fan and hilarious raconteur.

Indeed, a good majority of the 192 contributors herein say something about the man's famed sense of humor, whose pinpoint, spontaneous wit rivaled that of any professional humorist. His lines and his stories, liberally sprinkled throughout, will have you laughing until you gasp for what's left of breath. Start with the story he tells about Buddy Rich with Sam Most and the sextet in Chicago.

Jake Hanna, during the Concord Jazz record label years

Above all, of course, Hanna was a drummer, with legions of admirers in and out of the business. Drummers of every style and age—read Centerstram's *Charlie Watts' Favorite Drummers*–worshipped him. Though Judge's work is not an instructional book or educational manual, there's plenty of meat here for drummers about Hanna's style, philosophy, technique, drum tuning, the art of playing brushes and cymbals, his thoughts on equipment, and opinions on other drummers, musicians and singers. Though he revitalized the bands of Maynard Ferguson and Woody Herman much in the same way as Louie Bellson revitalized Duke's band, he was a superb small group player and accompanist to singers, was instrumental in the formation and ongoing success of the Concord Jazz label, was responsible for convincing Rosie Clooney to come back to the business, and set an example for jazz and for integrity by becoming the first player to leave a lucrative studio position to play jazz exclusively.

As just one example of how highly he was regarded in and out of the jazz community, when Bing Crosby returned to live performing for the last several years of his life, he only wanted one drummer backing him: Jake.

In describing Jake Hanna, two of the phrases that crop up again and again are "one of a kind," and "they don't make them like that anymore."

How true. But as funny as he was, to Jake Hanna, it was all about music.

Guitarist Howard Alden was right on the mark, saying, "...He was all about music. There was a sincerity and honesty in his playing, and if you played sincerely and honestly with him, he would like it and respect it. He had no tolerance for bullshit. When he played, he was behind every note, there was no trying to put on airs. He was completely in service of the music, the beauty and the swing.

"Jake was the most sincere, no-nonsense musician on any instrument, not just drums. Every note was from the heart and was full of integrity."

It's not certain whether awards are given out for books like these. If they're not, there should be. If they are, Maria S. Judge should win it. – *Backstage, 2012.*

"RIFFTIDE, THE LIFE AND OPINIONS OF 'PAPA' JO JONES."

Jonathan David Samuel Jones, aka "Papa" Jo Jones (1911-1985) was the father of modern jazz drumming. His trailblazing work with Count Basie's big band, first in 1934, then between 1936 and 1944, and again from 1946 to 1948, changed the drummer's function from that of foursquare timekeeper to sensitive accompanist. As a section player, Jones moved away from the four-to-the-bar bass drum beat and rudimentally-focused concentration on the snare drum, to an emphasis on the hi-hats—and later the larger "ride" cymbals—generally characterized by a lighter concept that was totally new to drumming.

Maybe the late Whitney Balliett, deemed "the poet laureate of jazz," said it best when he wrote that Jo Jones was "the man who played like the wind." If Gene Krupa made the drums a solo instrument, Jo Jones made the drums a musical instrument.

Rifftide: The Life and Opinions of Papa Jo Jones (University of Minnesota Press) is a modest work, as charming, quirky, and enigmatic as its subject. The book is based on a series of interviews with Jones that renowned writer Albert Murray conducted between 1977 and 1985. The tapes languished within Murray's archives until a 21-year-old college student named Paul Devlin, who worked for Murray mainly as a gofer, became aware of them and ultimately received Murray's permission to transcribe them for possible use in a book. By his own admission, Devlin, a non-musician, knew nothing of Jo Jones prior to getting started on this project.

Tremendously literate and well-read, Jones was a storyteller, righteous philosopher, and spinner of all manners of tall tales, though according to some who knew and worked with him, he was difficult to know and could be even more difficult to like. Several players simply avoided him. Others characterized him, especially later in life, as "mad." At the very least, Jo Jones kept his own counsel.

There's a good deal of boasting and tale telling within this narrative, and names are dropped by the dozen. But readers seeking revelatory insights about the personal and professional lives of the many legends with whom Jones worked, and the secrets of Jones' playing style and evolution, should look elsewhere. While he does speak of Duke Ellington, Basie, John Hammond, Ella Fitzgerald, and a bunch of others–he was particularly hard on Butch Miles, who was drumming with Basie when Albert Murray recorded these tapes–there's not a tremendous amount of depth to his comments. Drummers particularly will be disappointed, as there's very little in this book about drums, drummers, and drumming, and there is no discography or filmography.

Though it's easy to fault Murray for what's missing here–he did conduct the interviews, after all–Jones simply didn't answer questions in the conventional sense. He just talked. And talked. Ultimately, some information is to be gleaned, though never easily.

One suspects that Jones, who came up in the world of carnivals, medicine shows, and vaudeville, kept his bag of show business and musical tricks to himself–as most show people did back then–lest someone steal their secrets. Thank goodness his playing spoke for itself. Fortunately, we have the utterly remarkable audio recording from 1973 called The Drums by Jo Jones, where the master opens up musically and verbally about everyone from Baby Dodds to Krupa.

"Papa" Jo Jones with the early 1940s Basie trumpet section

Rifftide is not without its merits. An invaluable and lengthy afterword by jazz historian and broadcaster Phil Schaap, who knew Jones for 30 years, makes the man and the musician come alive. Schaap accurately explains Jones' art and contributions, and sensitively deals with the issue of his irascibility and his sometimes disconcerting interactions with his fellow musicians. Schaap clearly loved the man.

There have been other, sadly aborted attempts at an autobiography of Jo Jones, spearheaded by the likes of John Hammond, Preston Love, and Linda Kuehl. And in 1973 Milt Hinton conducted an extensive interview with Jones for the *Jazz Oral History Project*. While that interview can be accessed at Rutgers' Institute of Jazz Studies in Newark, the Project was NEA funded and that prohibits any profiting from the tape or the text. In other words, we'll likely never see that in book form.

Rifftide doesn't pretend to be anything other than it is, and disappointments notwithstanding, there is a good deal of charm to Jo Jones' wit and wisdom. As Phil Shaap suggests, "While the stories might be amusing, what makes them important is the fact that Jo Jones is the greatest drummer who ever lived. That's not just me talking. I stole that line from Max Roach. Every honest percussionist has quoted it, too." – *Modern Drummer magazine, 2011.*

JOE MORELLO (1928 – 2011)

Joe Morello, one of the greatest and most famous drummers of his time, died on March 12. He was 82.

On purely a technical basis, he was the equal of Buddy Rich and Louie Bellson. In terms of fame, he was a member of what could have been described, at the time, as the jazz equivalent of The Beatles: The Dave Brubeck Quartet. Morello was with Brubeck from 1956 until 1967. Dave Brubeck's group was among the most famous in jazz, even appealing to those who might have not liked jazz before or since.

Much of this was due to Morello. It was Paul Desmond's composition, "Take Five," featuring Morello's soloing, that was said to be the first, million-selling record in jazz history. And he won the prestigious DownBeat magazine poll as "Number One Drummer" in 1962, 1963 and 1964.

Born in Springfield, Massachusetts, in 1928, he first played violin before switching to percussion. He played in the New England area with Phil Woods, Sal Salvador, and in 1950, the big band of Glen Gray. Morello moved to New York City in 1952, making a name for himself in jazz circles with the bands of Johnny Smith, Gil Melle, and briefly with Stan Kenton. His three years with pianist Marian McPartland's trio, a group based at the Hickory House in New York City, from 1954 to 1956, really put him on the map. In 1956, he joined Brubeck.

From the start, Morello dealt with challenges that others did not. Though reports vary, it has been said that he was close to being blind for years. He lost whatever limited sight he had in 1976.

Joe Morello during his halcyon days with The Dave Brubeck Quartet

There were challenges with Brubeck as well, musically and otherwise. He clashed with alto saxophonist Desmond initially. Morello and his solos quickly became audience favorites, which did not thrill Desmond at all. Musically, Brubeck, bless his heart, had a tendency to rush, and it was up to Morello and bassist Gene Wright to "lock in" no matter what was happening, to keep Brubeck in tow.

Though Morello easily adapted to Brubeck's use of odd time signatures, but when the tune called for it, Joe could swing that band like mad. Listen to "Pennies from Heaven" on the Quartet's 1963 album recorded live at Carnegie Hall. You could swear it was Buddy Rich back there.

Joe Morello was probably the most famous teacher in drumming history. He toured extensively as a clinician for the Ludwig Drum Company, and Ludwig published many of Joe's method books. How Ludwig let him go and switch to the DW drum company is astonishing. In the 1960s, two drummers were responsible for selling thousands of Ludwig sets: Ringo to the would-be rockers, and Joe Morello to the jazz students.

He was one of the prime exponents of the controversial concept of "finger control"—whereby the movement and velocity of sticking is controlled by the fingers—and his many, many students swore by him. The great Danny Gottleib, possibly Joe's most famous student, idolized him. When I caught up with Dan in Philadelphia some years ago—he was backing the great jazz singer, Chris Connor—all he could talk about was Joe. He even offered to sponsor me if I studied with Morello.

Buddy Rich and Joe Morello, possibly at NYC's Manny's Drum Shop, early 1960s, where Dave Brubeck said Buddy and Joe "went at it all afternoon."

Despite his blindness, he remained very, very active in the post-Brubeck years. There were a few reunions with Brubeck, Marian McPartland and Sal Salvador, the participation in one of the first *Burnin' for Buddy* tribute recordings, a bunch of local gigs in the northern New Jersey area, and a very busy teaching practice.

Joe Morello was interviewed many times through the years in jazz and percussion journals, and always came off as a modest, self-effacing artist, though aware of his influence and place in history. He knew that the problems with his sight may have limited the scope of his career, if only because he couldn't take heavy reading gigs, but he was never bitter.

For those not familiar with his playing, check out his work with Brubeck, and on film and video via the DVDs *Legends of Jazz Drumming and Classic Drum Solos and Drum Battles.*

If anyone personified the title, "Legend of Jazz Drumming," it was Joe Morello. He was one of the great ones. *—Backstage, 2011.*

V
That's Showbiz

JERRY LEWIS

The drum-focused videos, now DVDs, I wrote and co-produced for DCI Music Video / Warner Bros.–later Hudson Music–had all done well, but after a period of time, it occurred to us that most of the folks buying these films about Buddy Rich, Gene Krupa, etc., were buying them for the drum solos. Ultimately, the individual and collective thought at Hudson Music was: Why not do a video featuring only drum solos, and if available, drum battles? There would be no payments to ASCAP or BMI for music rights, and with the focus on just the drum solos, we would actually be cutting right to the quick.

Jerry Lewis

Bear in mind that 15 years ago, there was no internet, and the availability of vintage drum solos on film was limited and hard to find. Nonetheless, the Hudson Music team–in this case, headed by yours truly-- managed to cobble together some great stuff, featuring solos from the likes of Rich, Krupa, Bellson, Philly Joe Jones, Papa Jo Jones, Max, Rufus Jones, Sam Woodyard, and a couple of neat battles from the Timex shows, etc. In the end, we were five minutes short, given that, in those days, if you didn't have 60 minutes worth of stuff, you had no video.

Enter Charley Braun, who, along with Louis Bernstein, Paul Testa, and a couple of overseas colleagues, have devoted a good deal of their lives to collecting Buddy Rich video, audio and other memorabilia. Braun parlayed his interest and his collection into the formation of the *International Buddy Rich Fan Club Newsletter*, which had thousands of subscribers all over the world, cluing fans and friends in about the newest discovery on film, tape, audio, and the rest. Charley actually didn't know what we were up to in terms of the production of *Classic Drum Solos and Drum Battles*, but by sheer coincidence, he called me at home, telling me about the existence of a Buddy Rich/ Jerry Lewis (!) drum battle, filmed circa 1955. None of us believed such a thing existed, but Charley got it to us the next day and sure enough, there it was, a comedic, Lewis/Rich drum duel filmed for *The Colgate Comedy Hour* television program. Not only was this an unbelievable find, it would put us over the essential, 60-minute running time.

Although *The Colgate Comedy Hour* television programs were and are in the Public Domain, it was common knowledge that Jerry Lewis could sometimes be problematic when it came to using film footage—with him in it—for commercial purposes without his permission. A letter—a plea, truth be told—was sent to his offices in Las Vegas, noting that most of our project were ultra-low budget affairs geared toward music students, and that we could only go as far as offering a small honorarium for permission to use the film. After hearing nothing after a few weeks, I came up with a new strategy: Resend the letter, but this time with a $200 check made out to Muscular Dystrophy enclosed.

A week later, on a Sunday morning at about 11:00 a.m., the phone rang in my Philadelphia home. It was Jerry Lewis. I couldn't believe it and still can't. Before he could say a word, I thanked him for being a positive influence on so many of us who decided to be in the entertainment industry, and also for all he had done for jazz over the years. He thanked me, and then in an utterly serious and straight forward manner, said the following: "I got your letter, and I know what you're doing. Not only am I going to give you permission to use the film you asked for, but I'm going to send you a box of VHS tapes of every appearance that Buddy Rich made on my telethons. And you can use any ones you want. The only thing I ask is that you let the Rich family know that I was of help." Jerry Lewis, by the way, is Cathy Rich's godfather. And please note, the box of tapes arrived three days later.

You hear stories about folks like Jerry Lewis, Mr. Sinatra, and various others, and not everything said is good. As for me, when legends like this step forward to contribute unselfishly and demonstrate the highest level of generosity when they really didn't have to, I won't believe or listen to anything negative. I only know how I was treated, and that's why I think Jerry Lewis is a great man. Happy 90th birthday, Jerry. *– Backstage, 2016.*

A DAY WITH MOE HOWARD (1897-1975)

The long-anticipated feature length film about The Three Stooges was released theatrically in 2012. For those who haven't seen it, or even for those that have, note that the Farrelly Brothers production is surprisingly good and often damn funny. Moe, Larry, Curly, Shemp, Joe Besser and Curly-Joe DeRita, rest their souls, would likely be pretty happy with it.

The film isn't about Stooge history. However, the true, latter-day story of the slapstick team is an extraordinary one.

In 1959 and 1960, the venerable, comedy trio was in the midst of one of the most miraculous comebacks in show business history. Almost washed up by 1958, when their 23-year Columbia Pictures contract for short subjects was cancelled, a number of television stations around the country purchased a bargain package of vintage Stooges' films offered by Columbia, often shown on children's shows in tandem with Popeye cartoons. No one had high hopes for these films, some produced as early as 1935. Edited Laurel and Hardy shorts didn't do well on television through the years, and silents went nowhere. Surprisingly, the kids went wild over the three comics and they gained an entirely new audience. Why? Cartoons were the basis of children's programming in those pre-*Sesame Street days*, and The Three Stooges were human cartoons, even in glorious black and white.

Moe Howard (1897-1975), who owned the act and the name, observed what was happening on television, ratings-wise, and because he just did not want to retire the act, he went into action. He knew that glued-to-the-television kids were making a lot of noise about wanting to see these guys in person, however elderly they were at that point. At the suggestion of Larry Fine, Moe hired a replacement "third stooge" by the name of Joe DeRita, who stepped in for Joe Besser. Besser ("You crazy, you") had served for a few years as the last "Curly replacement" in the Columbia film shorts. He didn't want to continue in the role, he claimed, as his wife was ill and he didn't want to travel. The truth is that Besser likely saw no future as a Curly Howard clone.

How wrong he ultimately turned out to be. The "new" Stooges, with DeRita in tow, had a tough time at first, having bombed out terribly at a club date in Bakersfield. Then things changed quickly.

DeRita shaved head ala the original Curly, was rechristened "Curly Joe," and The Stooges got a booking at what was one of this country's well-known nightclubs, now shuttered, the Holiday House in Pittsburgh, PA. The club's owner, egged on by *his* children, who loved The Stooges on television, hired the boys to do matinee shows, with the menu consisting of hamburgers, hot dogs and Cokes. The Holiday House was sold out for weeks. In 1959, the veterans were suddenly in demand for personal appearances, merchandising deals, comic books, recordings, television guest shots, and surprise of surprises, full-length feature films. No more shorts for these guys. Philadelphia television personality Sally Starr played The Stooges' short films on her highly-rated program, *Popeye Theater*, and one afternoon, Moe, Larry and Joe showed up in person on Starr's show and announced they would be appearing in a few weeks in Philadelphia at The Latin Casino nightclub.

Moe Howard

There was simply no question that I had to be there and nagged my folks—not Three Stooges fans, by the way—for weeks. They relented and I saw The Three Stooges in the flesh. They were, incidentally, as Moe used to say, "Even uglier in person." What kid wouldn't be unbelievably excited seeing these guys in person? I know I was, and I was so worked up that I did what any kid would do: I puked.

Fast forward to 1973. Larry Fine had suffered a stroke, Joe DeRita had retired after bombing with an act called "The New Three Stooges," and Moe was working as a single, initially on college campuses, where he showed vintage Stooge films and answered questions from the audience. Ultimately, he found new life doing his old routines on the popular Mike Douglas television show.

Left to right: Curly-Joe DeRita, Moe Howard, Emil Sitka, The Stooges that never happened

Howard was in Philadelphia for the Douglas program and for a gig at The TLA Cinema, a popular area theater, still in operation. At the time, I was a student at Temple University, a radio/television/film major, and trying vainly to get a writing position on the *Temple University News*. I was told by the newspaper's editor to "stand in line."

Knowing Moe was coming to town, my thought was, if I could get an exclusive interview with him and submit the story to the Temple newspaper, I'd *have* to be hired. After all, this was Moe. I used a contact I had at the local UHF television station, the station that was broadcasting Stooges' films daily, to help me set up an interview. The interview was scheduled at the theater for the early afternoon, and I made my way to the TLA.

I met Moe Howard and found him to be one of the most intelligent and gentle people I've ever met, in or out of the business. He was white-haired and about 74 years old then, but he was still Moe. Initially, I addressed him as "Mr. Howard," but he insisted I call him Moe. I told him I had been watching The Stooges on television every day since I was eight years old. "You've got a lot of courage, kid," he replied.

Given that I had a decent knowledge of show business by then, I figured that the only way to make my mark as a journalist was to use my smarts to come up with questions that were rarely asked. So, instead of asking Moe the usual, "Did you guys ever get hurt?" I opened with, "Moe, how long have you been working a single?"

He was impressed, and remarked that no one had ever asked him that before, and explained that after Larry's stroke and Joe DeRita's retirement, he finally had to break up the act. He loved working the colleges and got a kick out of the fact that all the students wanted was to get a pie in the face, thrown by the head Stooge. By the way, if you must know, the pies that The Stooges threw were filled with shaving cream.

After we were joined by his wife, Helen, Moe asked me about my interests. I told him of my drumming and interest in jazz. He then launched into a story about his friendship with Stan Kenton and how he insisted that Kenton be hired to appear in the Marine Ballroom of Atlantic City's Steel Pier during every Stooge Pier appearance in the main theater. Kenton and The Stooges? Who would have thought?

He did not hesitate to voice his bitterness about Abbott and Costello. Moe resented that A & C were doing full-length features for years, while The Stooges were stuck in Columbia's shorts department from 1935 to 1958. He believed that Costello was getting advance prints of Stooges' film shorts in order to copy the original Curly. If you can sit through the dross of most of Abbott and Costello's pictures, you'll see the validity of Moe Howard's claims.

We spent several marvelous hours together, and at the end of the interview, Moe presented me with the ultimate rarity: An autographed picture of Moe, Larry and the original Curly. I wrote my story and with autographed picture in hand, waltzed up to the offices of the *Temple University News*. Those in charge were astonished. I was hired instantly, and given carte blanche to write about whatever I wanted. I did interviews with everyone from Soupy Sales, Timothy Leary and Marilyn Chambers; to a feature on television's Superman, George Reeves; and a front-page obituary of Gene Krupa.

Am I grateful to Moe Howard for indirectly starting my long career as an editor, video producer, writer and author? Why soitenly!

About a year after my interview was published plans were made to resurrect The Three Stooges. Joe DeRita would return to the act, and long-time Stooge foil Emil Sitka ("hold hands, you lovebirds") would take the place of Larry. Moe blacked in his hair, photos were taken and there was a contract for a feature film appearance in the works. It never happened. Moe Howard died in 1975. His autobiography, *Moe Howard and The Three Stooges*, one of a load of books about the Stooges on the market, was published posthumously two years later. In 2000, a surprisingly good television movie about the Stooges was aired to great ratings. The Farrelly Brothers' feature stands as ample enough proof that the Stooges can—and will most likely—live forever. – *Backstage, 2009.*

GIA MAIONE: MRS. LOUIS PRIMA (1941-2013)

Throughout the 1970s, despite a memorable, three-year, on-and-off stint with influential organist Milt Buckner; a good portion of my musical life was spent drumming in society orchestras, and in "ham and egg" bar bands that churned out stuff like "Stagger Lee." There were a lot of requests for Louis Prima songs in those days, and though I had heard the name of Louis Prima, I wasn't familiar with his music. After I purchased his *Greatest Hits LP*, I was struck by musical lightning much in the same way I was when I first heard Charlie Ventura, Gene Krupa and Frank Sinatra.

Prima's post-1954 small groups ingeniously combined elements of early rock, rhythm and blues, New Orleans Dixie and Italian jive–backed by an infectious shuffle beat and tons of energy–that was irresistible. Fine art? No. But it swung, it was electric, and I wanted some of it for myself. The song that really got to me was something called "Just A Gigolo" coupled with "I Ain't Got Nobody."

My colleague and childhood friend Andy Kahn moved on from jazz piano playing, for the moment, anyway, into becoming owner of a busy and popular recording studio in Philadelphia, and later as a record producer and the man behind the 1978 number one dance hit, "Hot Shot." Kahn was so influential in the industry at the time, he was offered a lucrative contract by the RSO record label, owned by those responsible for the *Saturday Night Fever* film, among other things.

I had to take "Just a Gigolo" by this Louis Prima guy to Andy. I knew he would flip. Not only did he flip, but he suggested the absolutely outlandish: That he remake "Just a Gigolo," with yours truly, hardly a singer at the time, singing ala Louis Prima. To cut to the chase, my "interpretation" of Prima was decent, we recorded "Just a Gigolo" complete with original musical arrangement, RSO records loved it and had big plans to release it, promote it, and promote me.

Mrs. Louis Prima, Gia Maione, at her Destin, FL home

Then the bottom dropped out of the record business, seemingly overnight, and dozens of artists and producers involved in the disco movement saw their contracts cancelled and their careers ended. Hence, no "Just a Gigolo" sung by Bruce Klauber and produced by Andy Kahn.

Six or so years later, a rock singer named David Lee Roth recorded his version of Prima's "Just a Gigolo," complete with original arrangement, and sold millions of records. But wait! Those one or two "clams" present on the instrumental bridge of Roth's version were *the exact same clams* heard on my version of "Just a Gigolo." Turns out that David Lee didn't copy Prima's "Gigolo." He somehow got a hold of the master and copied our version. Strange but true, and only in show business.

Still, I remained a Prima fan, and was fascinated by his ability to reinvent himself and change with the times.

Some 30 years after the "Gigolo" situation, I wrote and published several positive pieces about Louis Prima's fifth and last wife, Gia Maione, which focused on the lack of recognition accorded her as singing replacement for Keely Smith, and what she did to preserve

Louis Prima's musical legacy. As a result of those articles, Maione, married to Prima from 1963 until his death in 1978, contacted me about possibly writing an "as told to" autobiography that would focus on her life with Prima. She wanted "to set the record straight" about her recently-won, decades-long lawsuits against Keely Smith in line with Prima's muddled will and Estate, and various misconceptions about her and her husband. While there was and is a Prima bio on the market, published by the University of Illinois Press and written by Gary Boulard, it is relatively incomplete and generally unsatisfying. After we came to terms, Maione insisted that I come to her Destin, FL home, at her expense, to conduct extensive interviews with her and go through the archives.

Happier days for Gia Maione around 1965 with Louis Prima and Frank Sinatra

The Maione compound was impressive, complete with nicely appointed guest house, where I resided for the five-day stay. Maione, who made it clear that she wasn't well at the time due to an unspecified illness or illnesses, arrived in her living room late each morning, well-dressed and well-coiffed, looking like a much older version of the pictures taken when she was in Prima's band. She was usually attended by her long-time companion/boy friend, identified to me only as "Frank." Days were spent watching rare, archival footage of Louis, Keely, Gia, Sam Butera and The Witnesses, on the programs of television shows hosted by Merv Griffin, Dean Martin and the like, that would make any nostalgia freak and Prima fan salivate.

Obviously, we spoke at length about her professional and personal relationship with Prima. Though many things she said had been oft-quoted in the press already–"I didn't know when adoration ended and love began," was one repeated comment–she opened up when discussing the constant care she gave to her husband who was in a coma for almost three years before he died (Prima's only visitors in three years, other than family, were Bill Cosby and Pee Wee Russell), as well as the details of the Keely Smith suit and various legal entanglements. Maione also expressed a good deal of bitterness about the attention given to Louis Armstrong as a jazz icon, as opposed to her late husband, who continues to be regarded mainly as a lounge act, despite his widespread popularity and, in some quarters, as an influence.

After not too long a time, it became apparent that hours of interviews with Gia Maione about visiting her comatose husband in the hospital and running to lawyers to battle Keely Smith, might not constitute lively book material. And boyfriend Frank's redneck references to Jews and blacks were making my stay in Destin, FL a bit uncomfortable. Still, I thought–while trying to think of a way to get the hell out of Destin as soon as possible–if I could speak later on to a dozen or so folks who knew and/or worked with Louis Prima, coupled with whatever useable material I got from Maione, there may be enough material for a decent book.

Upon my arrival back home in Philadelphia, I promptly rang up a number of folks who knew Louis, Keely, Gia and Sam Butera over the years. Names will go unmentioned here, but much to my surprise and horror, only two of them, Bobby Rydell and comic Tom Dressen, would respond at all to my requests for info. And I had known most of the celebs I called for years!

It dawned on me much later that these folks simply did not like the fact that Gia Maione battled and aired dirty laundry for 18 years about their much-beloved friend, colleague and fellow celebrity, Keely Smith. Who the hell was this Gia Maione, anyway? Didn't she start her career as a waitress at Howard Johnson's?

In the end and to her credit, Gia Maione facilitated the lucrative deal between retailer "The Gap" and use of Prima's "Jump, Jive and Wail" that revived the Prima brand; and at long last, made the post-1962 catalog of Louis Prima recordings done for his own "Magnagroove Records" available to the general public. But sadly, there was no book. No one wanted to talk. What is especially interesting is that, among the many Prima fans still out there, the perception is that Keely Smith is the widow of Louis Prima. Few have heard of anyone named Gia Maione.

Gia Maione died in Destin, FL in 2013 at the age of 72 due to unspecified circumstances. No word what happened to her friend, Frank. The two children Gia had with Louis Prima, Louis, Jr. and Lena, have become entertainers of a sort, singing and playing the music of their father. Truth be told, they're not very good. – *Backstage, 2013.*

PAT COOPER GOES CRAZY

During the time I was affiliated with singer Joanie Sommers, I was able to help get her booked at the Tropicana Hotel and Casino in Atlantic City in the main room, opening for the then-popular comic, Pat Cooper, real name, Pasquale Caputo. Joanie did well. Cooper, who I always sensed was a mean guy, naturally put the moves on her. Came with the territory then, I guess. I visited Joanie backstage after the show and she let me know that we were "all getting together" at the Trop's comedy club, then called "The Comedy Stop at the Trop," in an hour or so. The "we" consisted of Pat Cooper, comedian/actor Sal Richards, producer Dick Fox, who had found tremendous success as producer of the "Golden Boys of Bandstand" travelling show; Joanie Sommers and me.

The local comic on the bill at the comedy club was clearly excited when we all walked in, mainly about Pat Cooper, and introduced Cooper, Fox, Richards and Joanie from the stage. Comics, like jazz musicians, like to sit-in after hours or after their main shows. In its purest sense, comedy can be almost be a form of jazz. Sal Richards was invited to the stage first. The plan was that, after Richards completed a short comedy set, the star, Pat Cooper, would be asked to perform.

Pat Cooper

Sal Richards was and is a funny and hard-working actor and comic who has not yet received the widespread recognition he deserves. Mounting the stage, he went into his standard routine, which I'd heard several times. So did Pat Cooper.

Then Cooper began to yell from our table. "I don't want to hear your regular act," he shouted. "Let's hear some ad-libs, God dammit." The whole club laughed heartily, thinking this was all planned. Richards continued his act. So did Pat Cooper. "I don't want to hear this shit," Cooper shouted. "I told you, I want to hear some ad-libs. Can't you fucking ad-lib?"

Sensing that Cooper was really angry, the crowd was beginning to get uneasy, and Richards tried to resume. Then Cooper bolted up from our table and started running toward the stage, yelling and cursing obscenities at Sal Richards all the while. This was truly inconceivable. A famous performer was literally going nuts. In public. It was like witnessing a car wreck in slow motion.

Things finally calmed down to an extent, but there was a great deal of discomfort in the air. I was writing my "Backstage" column at the time for *Atlantic City* magazine and several others at the time, and I commented to Joanie Sommers that this would make one hell of a story. She looked me in the eye and said, "You will never write about this." Well, almost 25 years have passed since this incident, so I guess the story can finally be told.

I contacted Sal Richards not long ago to confirm that this scenario actually did happen. "It sure did," Richards said. "I'll never forget it."

"But why, Sal?" I asked. "Why would this guy do this?" Sal Richards' answer: "Because Pat Cooper is a fucking nut-bag."

Pat Cooper's autobiography, *How Dare You Say Dare Me?* was published in 2011. While reading it, I recalled that in his earlier days as a headliner and guest all over the airwaves, he was funny. Somewhere along the way, he became angry, often complaining in the media about the big money that headliners like Sinatra and Tony Bennett received as performers, claiming they were destroying the business. I never understood this, in that those he deemed "overpriced headliners" kept him in business for years. Maybe he was smarter than I thought. He formed an affiliation with radio bad boy Howard Stern, and aired his grievances often on the Stern program, gaining a younger audience in the process.

In 2013 at the age of 84, he publicly announced his retirement, saying, he was "too old to continue anymore." – *Backstage, 2011.*

PARTYING WITH NORMAN MAILER AND CHARLES MINGUS

In 1972, my friend Andy Kahn and yours truly performed in a musical group that we had the nerve to call "The All-Star Jazz Trio," and it's still swinging today. As detailed in this book's introduction, Kahn and I had been playing together since we were kids, with me on drums, and a number of bass players. By the time we turned 18, we had become decent jazz players. Well, enthusiastic ones anyway.

In 1971, there was virtually no live jazz to be heard in Center City Philadelphia, but that didn't stop us from approaching a restaurant/club– called "Skewers" and located on tony Rittenhouse Square–about presenting live jazz several nights a week. The short-lived gimmick of the restaurant was that all the food was served on a skewer, hence the name. If memory serves, Andy Kahn played solo piano the first night, I brought my drums down–for free–the next night, and the following night a bass player, who lived in the apartment building above the restaurant and had been enjoying us from the bar, joined us. As of that night, we were booked five nights per week, and it didn't take long for the whole enterprise to pick up steam.

Norman Mailer

All the real and wannabe jazz fans came out of hiding to hear these rambunctious, 18-year-olds, if only because Philadelphia jazz fans had nowhere to go after the demise of clubs like Peps, the Showboat and New Jersey's Red Hill Inn. It didn't take long for musicians to get the word about the action, and we had our share of well-known "sitters in," including Pepper Adams and Jerry Dodgian of the Thad Jones/Mel Lewis Jazz Orchestra, pianist Bernard Peiffer, Ronald Reuben and Glenn Dodson of the Philadelphia Orchestra (we later recorded with Reuben and Dodson), and on one evening, just about half of the Woody Herman Orchestra. We even hired our own press agent, who made sure our names appeared in the gossip columns regularly in exchange for a $25 per month fee.

Supporting us through the years in our musical endeavors was a dear, dear friend, who left us much too soon some years ago, named David Kay. Kay was not a jazz musician. He was a fan and listener who was exposed to the real stuff in New York City at a young age. His mother was jazz singer Carol Stevens, who recorded several impressive projects for Atlantic Records backed by jazz stars like Herbie Mann; did very well on the New York jazz club scene; and got some great write-ups in the trades and even in *Time* magazine. Since 1969, Stevens had been living with Norman Mailer, the literary giant and larger-than-life personality who passed away on November 10th of last year at the age of 84.

Charles Mingus

Always the publicity hound, which is why Mailer was as much a "personality" as he was a writer, he decided in February of 1973 to throw himself a 50th birthday bash. This would be no mere party. It would be held at the Four Seasons hotel in New York City with 550 of Norman Mailer's closest friends as invitees. In true Mailer style, he decreed that each and every one of the 550 people invited would have to pay $30 per person (then a hefty fee) to attend the bash. Evidently, all or most of them paid up, and the guest list included some major names, like Shirley MacLaine, Muhammad Ali and then-Senator Jacob Javits. A couple of somewhat lesser names were also on the guest list, courtesy of David Kay and his mother. Those names were Andy Kahn and Bruce Klauber. And we didn't have to pay the $30 admission fee.

I have no recollection of just how we got to New York. I suspect it was either in Kahn's Fiat or my Vega. However we did get there, what we witnessed upon our arrival at The Four Seasons was absolutely incredible. People were jammed in everywhere, and there were big stars at every turn. The crowd was buzzing in anticipation of Mailer's remarks that were to be made later that evening. He was supposed to be saying something of major, international consequence (long-time Mailer foe Gore Vidal once commented that everything Mailer ever said in public was supposed to be of major consequence).

Kahn and I were greeted by our friend David Kay, his mother, and surprise of surprises, the "Man of the Hour" in person. Mailer was quite gracious, and said something to the effect that he heard of the fine work we were doing as young jazz musicians, and that he understood us to be "quite talented." I don't remember whether or not he patted us on the head.

Then the music began, and this was music of the real, all-star variety. The players included baritone saxophonist Pepper Adams, who had kind of taken Andy and I under his wing when he played with us in Philadelphia; composer/multi-instrumentalist David Anram; and the legendary bassist /composer Charles Mingus. Pepper Adams tried to make us feel comfortable and at home. I think he realized that one of us–that would be me–was in way over his head that night. Andy Kahn, who had been in show business since childhood, was not in over his head. He was in his element.

One of the many real novelties of the evening had to do with just how the food was served. This night, guests were invited to get whatever they wanted, from desserts to appetizers to entrees, direct from The Four Seasons kitchen and eat in the kitchen if they so desired. None other than Charles Mingus himself made sure that Andy and Bruce, the two young jazzers from Philadelphia, were escorted properly into the Four Seasons kitchen. Mingus suggested that we all dine on apple pie, which he deemed "the best in the world." It was, and the Charles Mingus who was said to be among the most volatile personalities in the music world, was not on view that evening.

Then it was time for the birthday boy's big speech, the one that would be of major, international consequence. Mailer sauntered up to the microphone in front of 550 adoring fans. It soon became clear, however, that the honoree may have downed too many bourbons too quickly.

The notoriously anti-feminist Mailer began his remarks thusly: "A lot of people ask me," he said after the applause had died down after his introduction, "why I associate with so many worn-out, older women. Well, I'll tell you why. Because they're all the same once you get past the old, worn-out part." Hoo boy. And that was just the start of it.

His remarks only went further downhill from there. Mostly, he was rambling semi-incoherently, and the portion that was supposed to be of major consequence had vaguely to do with a citizen's agency that he wanted to set-up to investigate the CIA. He called it "The Fifth Estate," or something like that.

The evening seemed to slowly deflate after that, but the partying, eating and drinking continued long into the night, though not with the same fervor. I was ready to leave. Andy Kahn, bless his heart, wanted to stay until morning.

I again have no recollection as to when we got back to Philadelphia and how we got there. What I did know was that we had a once-in-a-lifetime experience that defined jazz and defined New York City during those great days.

I wish I had a photograph of that night, but I do have one memento. Our press agent certainly worked overtime for us in this case. A day or two after the party, an item appeared in the entertainment column of the *Philadelphia Inquirer* that read in part, "Andy Kahn and Bruce Klauber of The All-Star Jazz Trio playing at Skewers, were Philadelphia representatives and invited guests at Norman Mailer's 50th birthday party held at New York CIty's Four Seasons hotel."

It's true. I still have the press clipping. Yep. Andy and Bruce were there. – *ICON magazine, 2012.*

Note: Norman Mailer died in 2007 at the age of 84. Charles Mingus was 56 when he passed in 1979.

First Ending

I've been asked the following questions rather often for decades. Hopefully, this will set the record straight:

1) When will the entire Benny Goodman Carnegie Hall Jazz Concert of January 16, 1938 be out on video?
Answer: It won't. Video did not exist in 1938 and unless we find out otherwise, brief newsreel footage is the only filmed evidence in existence of this landmark performance.

2) Who was the better drummer, Gene Krupa or Buddy Rich?
On a technical basis, no one can – and most likely, no one ever will – come close to what Buddy Rich could do on the drums. If Superman played drums, it would have been Buddy Rich. Krupa brought something else to the table: He made the drums a solo instrument, brought drums to the forefront, and in his appearances in 26 films and dozens of radio and television appearances, proved that a jazz musician could also be a media personality. And we'll never know how many youngsters took up the drums because of Gene. I'm certainly one of them.

3) What was Benny Goodman really like?
I called the Goodman office in the early 1980s in order to see about setting up a brief phone interview in conjunction with the book I was writing about Gene Krupa. After his secretary put me on hold, The King himself unexpectedly picked up the phone and caught me off guard when he asked what kind of questions about Gene I would want to ask him. Thinking on my feet, I asked, "Well, Mr. Goodman, you played with Gene at the beginning of his career and you played with him close to the end of his career. How would you say his accompaniment had changed?" Goodman's answer: "I'd say he was rather consistent. He was in my band of course, and you have all the records. Then he formed his own band, which was rather successful. When did you say he died?" My reply: "In 1973. He was 64 years old." Goodman's reply: "My, what a shame." Then he hung up the telephone. And that was what Benny Goodman was really like.

Second Ending

When he was a college student who aspired to a career in show business, Dick Cavett accidently ran into television producer and writer John ("One Step Beyond") Newland on a New York City street corner. Cavett endeavored to chat up Newland, spoke of his personal showbiz aspirations and asked Newland for advice. Newland answered Cavett only by saying, "Showbiz. It's a rotten damned game."

I don't agree. I've loved every moment of it. Okay, every moment of it that wasn't rotten.

A, A♯/B♭, B, C, C♯/D♭, D, D♯/E♭, E, F, F♯/G♭, G, G♯/A♭

At CENTERSTREAM Publishing we've got these arranged in ways that can make you cry, burn, shred, giggle, love, hate, explore, wonder, ponder, and understand. It's astonishing what those 17 little notes can do.

In Dave Celentano's hands he shreds them, Ken Perlman's banjo wound them into melodic songs. Joe Weidluch's guitar twisted them into jazz patterns. Brian Emmel's bass slapped them into shape, Jorge Polanuer's sax put them into classic songs, Tom Ball's harmonica blew them into old familiar patterns, Max Palermo's bass exercises made them the ultimate, Ron Middlebrook turned them into a best seller, Kenny Sultan's guitar put them in the blues, and Glen Caruba pounded his drums into new grooves with them. Find out what these little notes have done for others and can do for you, send for your Centerstream catalog today.